Wolfgang Amadeus Mozart

Musician

by Carol Greene

CHILDRENS PRESS®
CHICAGO

DEDICATION

This book is for Deborah Carter

PICTURE ACKNOWLEDGMENTS

Historical Pictures Service, Inc., Chicago—Cover (inset), frontispiece, pages 8, 30, 44, 70 (2 photos), 71 (3 photos), 72 (2 photos), 73 (3 photos), 74 (2 photos), 75 (2 photos), 76, 92
Cover illustration by Len W. Meents

Library of Congress Cataloging in Publication Data

Greene, Carol.
  Wolfgang Amadeus Mozart: musician.

  Includes index.
  Summary: A biography of the man who may be the greatest musical genius of all time.
  1. Mozart, Wolfgang Amadeus, 1756-1791—Juvenile literature. 2. Composers—Austria—Biography—Juvenile literature. [1. Mozart, Wolfgang Amadeus, 1756-1791. 2. Composers] I. Title.
ML3930.M9G73 1987   780′.92′4 [B]   87-13824
ISBN 0-516-03261-5

Table of Contents

Chapter 1
Wolferl   9

Chapter 2
The Wonder Children   15

Chapter 3
The Grand Tour   21

Chapter 4
Growing Pains   31

Chapter 5
A Warm Welcome   37

Chapter 6
The Cage   45

Chapter 7
Job Hunting   51

Chapter 8
Love and Tragedy   57

Chapter 9
Trials and a Trap   63

Chapter 10
   Beginnings   77

Chapter 11
   Family Life   85

Chapter 12
   Friends   93

Chapter 13
   The Prague Connection   99

Chapter 14
   Debts and Depressions   105

Chapter 15
   "Lacrymosa"   111

Chapter 16
   Afterwards   117

Time Line   120

Index   123

Chapter 1

WOLFERL

Icy winter winds shrieked down from the mountains and chased one another through the streets of Salzburg. Snow hung like sugar frosting from homes, shops, and churches. Fountains stood frozen and still, and above all the twelfth-century fortress, Hohensalzburg, kept watch like a giant bear. It was almost eight o'clock on Sunday evening, January 27, 1756.

But in a back room on the third floor at 9 Getreidegasse, no one was thinking about the weather. There Anna Maria Mozart struggled to give birth to her seventh child. Her husband, Leopold, and kind neighbors tried to help. They all knew that five Mozart babies had already died. Only Anna Maria's second child, four-year-old Nannerl (a nickname for Maria Anna), had survived.

At last the new baby arrived. He was so small and frail that his chances for survival did not look good. So the very next morning he was bundled up and rushed to the Salzburg cathedral to be baptized. His official name was almost bigger than he was: Johannes Chrysostomus Wolfgangus Theophilus Mozart.[1] His family called him Wolferl.

How proud Papa Leopold must have felt when he looked at his new little son. How he hoped this baby would live. After all, if Leopold's family had had their way, there wouldn't be any Wolferl—or Nannerl either.

Wolferl's great-great-grandfather, David Mozart, had been a master mason in Bavaria. His youngest son, Franz, followed the same trade. Franz's son, Johann Georg, worked as a bookbinder. When it came time for Johann Georg to choose a profession for his son, Leopold, he decided the boy should become a priest.

So young Leopold set out to study. But before long he fell in love—with music. Soon he could think of nothing else. He learned to play the violin and various keyboard instruments. He even composed music of his own.

At last his superiors at the university expelled him for cutting too many classes. That didn't bother Leopold. In 1743, when he was twenty-four, he became fourth violinist in the court orchestra of Count Sigismund von Schrattenbach, the prince-archbishop of Salzburg. Finally he was doing what God meant him to do. He was a musician.

1. Theophilus is a Greek name that means "beloved of God." Later, Wolfgang decided that he liked the Latin form of his name, Amadeus, better.

Four years later, Leopold married Anna Maria Pertl, a cheerful, pretty young woman who had been living with her widowed mother in Salzburg. The newlyweds made their home in the third-floor apartment of a cream-colored house at 9 Getreidegasse. Folks called them "the handsomest couple in Salzburg." True, Leopold could be bossy at times. But Anna Maria didn't seem to mind, and friends loved to visit their warm, happy home.

Now here lay little Wolferl. What a welcome addition he would be to the family, if he lived. Well, thought the Mozarts, folks said that sugar water was better for babies than milk. They had tried it with Nannerl and it had worked. They might as well try it with the new baby too.

Maybe the sugar water did work. Or maybe Wolferl was just tougher than he looked. In any case, he did live and grew into a bright, lively little boy. He was a good child too.

Leopold Mozart did not earn a large salary, but his family was comfortable. They had enough to eat and big stoves of porcelain and tile to keep them warm during the long Salzburg winters. The family's pet bird, Herr Canari, trilled away in his cage and Anna Maria's cheerfulness animated everyone around her.

The Mozarts loved one another too, and were not afraid to show it. That was especially important to Wolferl. From person to person he would run. "Do you love me?" he would ask again and again.

Of course his family usually said yes. But the Mozarts enjoyed being silly too. So sometimes they said no, just to see what would happen. It was always the same. Little Wolferl would burst into tears, and wouldn't stop crying until he was absolutely positive that everyone in his family loved him as much as he loved them.

Most of all, he adored his stern-faced papa.

"Nothing ventured, nothing gained," Leopold would preach in an important-sounding voice. "God will make everything right." And, sometimes, "It's all up to God, but we can help Him . . ."

Wolferl was impressed. "Next to God comes Papa," he said.

At bedtime, he and Leopold played a special game. Wolferl had made up a little song with nonsense words. Every night he stood on a chair and sang it with his father. Then he kissed his father and promised to keep him in a glass case when he grew old. Out from under their parents' big bed came Wolferl and Nannerl's little trundle beds and the two children settled down for sleep.

Naturally music was important in the Mozart home. After all, it was Leopold's job. But it was more than that too. Sometimes he brought his fellow musicians from court back to the apartment with him. Together they played trios or quartets or just sat and talked about music.

When Nannerl was seven, Leopold began giving her lessons on the clavier.[2] She was talented, he discovered, surprisingly talented. But Leopold didn't realize that three-year-old Wolferl, sitting on the floor nearby, had an even bigger surprise in store for him.

Closer and closer to the clavier crept the little boy. His father and sister paid no attention to him. When Nannerl's lesson was over, he reached up with his fat baby fingers and played some notes that sounded pretty to him. How beautiful! But all of a sudden he hit two notes that didn't sound right together. Then Wolferl wailed. Music shouldn't sound like *that*, he knew.

For a while, Leopold just watched his son and wondered. By the time Wolferl was four, though, Papa thought he should start lessons too. Before long, the boy could memorize little pieces and play them perfectly.

But after a while that wasn't enough for Wolferl. He wanted to make up his own pieces. Fine! said Leopold; he would write them down. So the young child composed his first work, a minuet in G. (K. 1).[3]

Soon he decided to write a concerto.[4] The music was very difficult, Wolferl explained to his father, because that was

2. The clavier is an ancestor of the piano.
3. The K stands for Köchel. In 1862 Ludwig von Köchel published a catalogue that chronologically organized and numbered Wolfgang's compositions.
4. A concerto is a composition, in three contrasting movements, for one or more soloists and orchestra.

how concertos were supposed to be. And the manuscript was rather messy because Wolferl had written down the notes himself with pen and ink. So what if he couldn't write words yet? Music was what counted with him.

At first, Leopold thought the concerto was just a mess of ink blots. But after he had studied it, he said, "This child has not only written a concerto, but one so difficult that nobody can possibly play it."

The year his son was born, Leopold had published a book about how to play the violin.[5] Now Wolferl wanted to learn that instrument too. So his proud papa got him a small violin all his own and watched him work away at it.

There was only one problem with teaching Wolferl, said Leopold. He seemed to know everything already. What on earth would be next?

5. It is still in print today.

Chapter 2

THE WONDER CHILDREN

Soon Leopold answered that question himself. In those days, all Europe loved specially gifted children. German-speaking people called them *Wunderkinder*—wonder children—and Germany seemed to produce an unusually large crop of them.

Earlier in the eighteenth century, a little boy from Lübeck, Christian Heinrich Heinecken, amazed everyone who met him. He learned to talk when he was ten months old. By the time he was three, he could speak German, French, and Latin. His special field was religion and he spoke intelligently about it in all three languages. Poor Christian Heinrich died when he was four.

From the town of Schwabach came Jean-Philippe Baratier. At the age of five, he knew German, French, Latin, and Greek. Then he learned Hebrew, Arabic, and a few more Eastern languages. When he was twelve, he translated a book from Hebrew to French. Then he turned to mathematics and, after that, law. Jean-Philippe was a little luckier than Christian Heinrich. He lived to the age of eighteen.

Music also had its wonder children. Gertrud Elisabeth Schmeling was just seven years older than Wolferl. At the age of four, she picked up a violin and began to play scales. She had never had a lesson. Soon her father arranged for her to give concerts. Gertrud could sing too and grew up to become an internationally famous soprano.

When Wolferl was almost six and Nannerl ten, Leopold could wait no longer. After all, he had *two* wonder children to show the world. Time to get busy! So, in January 1762, he asked his prince-archbishop for a leave of absence, packed up his two little geniuses, and whisked them off to Munich, capital of Bavaria.

It was not an easy journey. Travel in those days was slow, uncomfortable, and sometimes even dangerous. Since the Mozarts did not own a coach, they either had to rent one or go by the mail coach or the commercial stagecoach. It took skilled men to drive the four horses over bumpy roads of mud or ice. Seven miles per hour was the fastest anyone could hope to go.

Travelers set off before sunrise and jounced along all day. Occasionally they had to stop for a fresh team of horses. Sometimes their coach broke down and they had to walk. At night they staggered into an inn for some food and a bed. Often they had to share the bed with hungry insects. The next day, the whole process began again. But, thought Leopold, it would be worth all the trouble if he could get his children off to a good start in the world of music.

Leopold and the children spent three weeks in Munich. They visited the court and the children played for the Elector[1] Maximilian Joseph III. Then they returned to Salzburg and stayed home for nine months. Still, Leopold must have been pleased with Wolferl and Nannerl, because in September he got them ready for another journey. This time he took the whole family to Vienna.

Their first stop was in Passau, where the local bishop was so impressed that he made them stay and perform for five days. For all this work, he gave them the puny reward of one ducat (about $12.50). *That* certainly didn't please Leopold.

But the concert at Linz went much better. Two noblemen who heard it promised to travel ahead and tell everyone in Vienna about the fabulous Mozart children. At the monastery of Ips, the monks all left their dinner to hear Wolferl play the organ. Then came a boat trip on the Danube River and, at last, Vienna.

Back then, Europe was divided into many little states, city-states, duchies, and other political sections. Each had its borders and its customhouses where weary travelers devel-

---

1. An elector was a German prince with special status in the Holy Roman Empire.

oped huge headaches while officials poked and prodded through their baggage. The same thing could have happened to the Mozarts as they entered Vienna. But Wolferl saved the day. He whipped out his child-sized violin and played a minuet.[2] The officials were so charmed that they passed the family right through. They didn't even charge them the usual fee.

The Mozarts were used to living around beautiful buildings in Salzburg. But their mouths must have fallen open when they first saw Vienna, Austria's capital. It was an old city with a long history. It was also the seat of power; a glittering, breathtaking city. Elegant palaces rose one after another. Towering above them all stood Saint Stephen's Cathedral, a glorious hodge-podge of architectural styles.

For musicians, Vienna was one of the three great cities of the world.[3] Operas, ballets, symphonies,[4] chamber music,[5] and religious works all delighted the Viennese. But, strangely enough, they thought the very best music had to be written and performed by Italians. In fact, the Viennese got more excited about Italian music than the Italians themselves did. Many years would pass before they truly recog-

2. Music for a slow, graceful dance popular at that time.
3. The other two were Paris and London.
4. Musical compositions written for an orchestra.
5. Music intended to be performed in a private room or a small concert hall.

nized their own great composers, such as Franz Joseph Haydn and Wolfgang Amadeus Mozart.

Even so, the noblemen had kept their promise and Vienna couldn't wait to meet the little Mozarts. Both Maria Theresa, empress of Austria, and her husband, Francis I, the Holy Roman Emperor, loved music. They commanded Leopold to bring his children to them on October 13.

So out to Schönbrunn Palace, south of the city, trooped the Mozarts. It was an incredible place with fourteen hundred rooms and vast grounds. The Mozarts stayed three hours and the children performed beautifully. Francis even called Wolferl "a little conjuror."

According to one story, Wolferl slipped and fell on the polished floor during his visit. Maria Antoinette, one of the empress's many children who was just about his age, helped him up. Wolferl was so grateful that he promptly asked her to marry him. Many years later, that same little archduchess had grown up to become Queen Marie Antionette of France and was beheaded by the guillotine during the French Revolution.

Maria Theresa and her husband gave Leopold a generous sum of money and the children presents, including formal state costumes they could wear at court. Nannerl's was ornamented white brocaded taffeta and Wolferl's lilac and gold. Later, Leopold had their portraits painted in their new finery.

After the visit to Schönbrunn, invitations poured in for the Mozarts. One aristocratic family after another sent its carriage to deliver the young performers and their papa in style. It was all a great deal of fun, but rather hard on a six year old, too. One day Wolferl came down with scarlet fever and the Viennese had to do without him until he recovered.

By December, though, he felt much better and the Mozarts set off for a concert in Pressburg. Then it was back to Vienna to play at Countess Kinsky's feast and finally, early in January, home to Salzburg.

For some months, Wolferl and Nannerl slept in their own trundle beds and ate Anna Maria's good cooking. Wolferl worked hard at his violin. But all the while, ideas were ticking away in Leopold's mind. The children had done so well in Vienna. Why not plan another trip? This time, though, they would travel by private coach. Leopold wasn't planning any small journey. He felt they were ready for a grand tour of Europe.

Chapter 3

THE GRAND TOUR

Today some people might say that Leopold Mozart was a bad father. Why would he drag his poor children across Europe and force them to perform? They should have been taking daily lessons or out playing with other children. Obviously, Leopold cared about nothing except money.

But it is not fair to judge people of other times and places by our standards. Leopold believed he was doing the best he could for his family. In his situation, he was probably right.

In those days, most musicians were treated as servants. Any nobleman worth his salt had some sort of music program at his court and hired performers and composers just as he hired cooks and gardeners. Leopold himself had that kind of job with the prince-archbishop of Salzburg. He knew that a steady post at a good court was exactly what young Wolfgang would need some day. The more important people he impressed and the more publicity he got as a child, the better his chances would be in the future.

Leopold didn't let his children go without lessons either. He taught them himself. Wolferl loved mathematics and was very good at it. Stories say that he used to scribble rows of figures all over paper, tablecloths, and even wallpaper. He also learned languages easily, especially Italian. During Nannerl's journeys, she kept a diary. In it she wrote in the language of whatever country she happened to be visiting. Naturally, both children picked up a lot about geography. And Leopold didn't have to force them to perform. They loved doing that best of all.

So, on June 9, 1763, the whole family climbed into their coach and set out. They had only been gone about a day, though, when the coach broke down at Wasserburg. Repairs would take at least a day. Other seven-year-old boys might whine and fret at such a delay. But not Wolferl. He found a "real" organ with pedals in the town and sat down to learn to play it. There was just one problem. His feet wouldn't reach the pedals. So he shoved the stool aside and stood on the pedals.

At Munich, the elector took a long time to pay for his concert, which made the Mozarts angry. But at Augsburg they gave three successful performances and visited their relatives too. Duke Carl Eugen at Ludwigsburg said he didn't want to hear the children. But Elector Palatine Carl Theodor at Schwetzingen wanted a four-hour concert.

From city to town to summer palace the family traveled.

Every so often, Leopold wrote home to Lorenz Hagenauer, his friend and landlord.

"Our concert was upon the 18th," he wrote from Frankfurt on August 20, 1763. "It was good. Everybody was astonished. By the grace of God we are in health, God be Praised, and are everywhere objects of admiration. As to our Wolfgangerl, he is extraordinarily gay, but naughty too."

That concert on the eighteenth went so well that Leopold decided to schedule three more in Frankfurt. A press release he wrote told what to expect at the last of the three.

"The little girl, who is in her twelfth year, will play the most difficult compositions of the greatest masters; the boy, who is not yet seven [he *was* seven!], will perform on the clavecin[1] or harpsichord[2] . . ."

"The boy" would also play a violin concerto and accompany symphonies on the clavier while the keyboard was covered with a cloth. People could play notes while he wasn't looking and he would name them. And he would improvise (make up) music in any key on the organ or harpsichord for as long as anyone wanted.

At one of those concerts sat a fourteen-year-old boy, enchanted by all he saw and heard. He grew up to be one of Germany's greatest writers, Johann Wolfgang Goethe. Many

1. The French word for harpsichord.
2. An instrument similar to a grand piano, but usually having two keyboards and two or more strings for each note.

years later, he told a friend how impressed he had been by "the little man with wig and sword."

On through Germany lumbered the Mozart coach, headed toward Brussels, then Paris. At Aix-la-Chapelle, Princess Amalia of Prussia tried to talk Leopold into coming to Berlin too. But Leopold didn't think that made much sense financially. If the kisses she gave the children were gold coins, he grumbled, it might be a different story.

Brussels brought financial headaches too. The prince kept putting off the concert.

"Indeed, it looks as though all were in vain," wrote Leopold, "for his highness the prince does nothing but hunt, gobble, and swill, and we may in the end discover that he has no money."

People did give the children valuable presents, such as snuff boxes and leather cases. But Leopold didn't think it would be tactful to sell these right away, so he shipped them home to Salzburg.

Finally the concert took place and the Mozarts could move on to Paris. Once again they found themselves in a colorful, bustling capital. They had plenty of letters of recommendation too. But, no one seemed interested in them. Cold November rains drenched the city and sodden filth littered the streets. Leopold had to hire sedan chairs to carry his children through the muck from one aristocratic home to the next, precious letters in hand. "Ho hum," seemed the general response.

Finally one letter remained. It introduced the Mozarts to Friedrich Melchior Grimm, a German who had lived in Paris for fifteen years. Grimm knew a good thing when he saw it. He took the Mozarts under his wing and by Christmas Eve had them at the court of King Louis XV at Versailles. They were to stay two weeks.

Their eyes must have bugged out when they saw how French royalty lived. True, Maria Theresa made sure everyone there led a normal family life. Here the king had one apartment, the queen and her daughters another, and the king's mistress, Madame Pompadour, still another. Folks crept through the palace halls at all hours on their way to secret love affairs that everyone knew about. Nobody smelled very clean.

The Mozarts were used to cold, but this place was the worst they had ever visited. Why, sometimes the wine even froze at the dinner table! On New Year's Day, the royal family gave them a special treat. They were allowed to stand behind the king and queen as they ate their dinner. Occasionally the queen turned around, handed Wolferl a bit of food, and murmured to him in German. What an honor!

But the king's three daughters hugged the young Mozarts and played with them. The family's stay at Versailles helped them in Parisian music circles too. Suddenly invitations from aristocrats fluttered in and the closed doors opened wide. Nannerl performed brilliantly and everyone marveled at Wolferl's improvisations. He also wrote four sonatas for clavier and violin in Paris. Two he dedicated to Madame Victoire, one of the king's kind daughters.

Wolferl heard a great deal of music and met some composers during his stay in France. But he never liked French music all that much. The real musical treats, as far as he was concerned, still lay ahead—in England.

Leopold hadn't been too sure about visiting London. His new friends in Paris talked him into it. The trip didn't begin well either. The regular boat across the English Channel was full, so he had to hire a special one. Rough water caused the whole family to make "a heavy deposit in vomiting," he wrote Hagenauer later.

But on April 22, 1764, they had docked in England and by April 27 had been presented to King George III and Queen Charlotte. The royal couple invited them back on May 19 to perform for a small group of friends. In another letter to Hagenauer, Leopold told how Wolferl sight-read pieces by several composers, including George Frideric Handel[3], accompanied the queen while she sang an aria[4] and then a flutist as he played a solo, and made up new music to go with the bass line of a Handel aria.

---

3. Handel was a famous German-born composer who was a British national.
4. A solo voice composition

"In a word," gushed Leopold, "what he knew when we set out from Salzburg was a mere shadow compared with what he knows now. It is beyond all conception."

Leopold realized that this was not the best time for a public concert in London. Most music lovers had already left the city for their summer homes. But, thought the wily father, they would be back on June 4 for the king's birthday. So he scheduled his concert for June 5. It was a smart move. They earned over twenty-six hundred dollars. Furthermore, most of the orchestral musicians who played with Wolferl and Nannerl refused to accept their usual fee. They felt it was a privilege to accompany such children.

Needless to say, Leopold planned many more public concerts during the stay in England. He also advertised them in ways bound to get people's attention. One notice began:

"To all Lovers of Sciences. The greatest Prodigy that Europe, or that even Human Nature has to boast of, is without Contradiction, the little German Boy WOLFGANG MOZART; a Boy, Eight Years old [he was nine by then], who has, and indeed very justly, raised the Admiration not only of the greatest Men, but also of the greatest Musicians in Europe."

Meanwhile, the prodigy was learning more about his art. Of course Handel's music impressed him. But he liked Johann Christian Bach even better. Christian, youngest son of Johann Sebastian Bach, had made his home in England by then and was happy to meet with young Wolfgang. Once the two sat together on an organ bench, the boy between Christian's knees. One would play for a while, then the other would take over. Listeners couldn't tell the difference.

Wolferl didn't neglect his composing either. During his time in England, he wrote six sonatas for clavier with violin or flute (K. 10-15), two symphonies (K. 16 and 19), a chorus (K. 20), and many smaller pieces. Some scholars think his father—or even Christian Bach—helped him with these. Christian certainly did influence the style of Wolferl's music. But it doesn't really matter if the boy had some grown-up help or not. His early compositions are still amazing.

The Mozarts ended up staying in England for over a year. There were some unhappy moments when one or another of them got sick. For a while, Leopold suffered from "a kind of native complaint which they call a *cold*." It must have been a bad one, because poor Leopold worried about what would happen to his children if he died.

But on the whole, the family had a good time. They saw such sights as Canterbury Cathedral and the Tower of London, where the roaring lions "frightened our Master Wolfgang exceedingly." They even attended a horse race. But finally it was time to move on. Princess Caroline in Holland wanted to hear the children and the prince-archbishop wrote that he would appreciate it if Leopold got himself back to Salzburg and his job.

So, in July 1765, the Mozarts crossed the English Channel again, this time "with a healthy stomach." But they didn't rush back to Salzburg. First Holland had to have its concerts. There Nannerl became ill, probably with typhus, and almost died. Princess Caroline sent her own doctor to save her. Then Wolfgang caught intestinal typhoid. What with illness and performances, the family couldn't leave Holland until the next April. Then they performed their way through France, Switzerland, and Germany.

Not until the end of November 1766 did they rumble back into Salzburg, home at last after almost three-and-a-half years.

Wolfgang performs with his father and sister in Paris, 1763

Chapter 4

GROWING PAINS

The prince-archbishop was not happy. What right, he muttered, did that Mozart fellow have to go traipsing off for years and years? His job was here, in Salzburg. Well, he would find a nasty little surprise waiting for him when he got back.

Actually, the surprise probably wasn't as nasty as Leopold feared. At least the prince-archbishop hadn't fired him. Instead, he had simply stopped paying him. From now on, Sigismund decreed, Leopold would get a salary only when he was in Salzburg—working. It wasn't such an unreasonable rule.

Furthermore, the prince-archbishop did not believe all this poppycock about young Wolfgang. The child could perform. Anyone with ears knew that. But those compositions? Much too advanced for a boy of his age. Leopold must have had a hand in them.

Maybe he had and maybe he hadn't. But Leopold did

realize that his son needed more work in the basics of composition. So as soon as they had settled in, he put him to work at counterpoint.[1] Wolfgang thoroughly enjoyed himself. Soon he was naming the different voices—Mrs. d'Alto, Duke Basso, and so on.

He also composed the music for the first act of an oratorio[2], *The Obligation of the First and Foremost Commandment* (K. 35). Next came a cantata,[3] performed during Lent. After that he wrote music to go with a Latin play put on by university students. He had the most fun after it ended, though, and he got to play the clavier in front of everyone for hours.

There was just one problem, Wolfgang thought. He was running out of music to play, especially with an orchestra. So he wrote four concertos for clavier and orchestra (K. 37 and 39-41). But he didn't start from scratch. Instead, for many sections, he borrowed music from other composers and arranged it into concerto form. This wasn't unusual, especially for busy performers who got tired of playing the same old things.

Meanwhile, in spite of the prince-archbishop's warnings, Leopold had his mind on another trip. If the old man didn't

1. Counterpoint is the study of how voices or parts should blend in a piece of music.
2. An oratorio is a long, dramatic work for voices and orchestra on a religious subject.
3. A cantata is a shorter piece for voices and instruments. It can be on a religious or a secular subject.

like it, too bad. As the father of a wonder child, he had to do what was best for his son's career.

Leopold's own career probably did suffer as a result of all he did for Wolfgang, but he felt the child must come first. About then, it just so happened that the Archduchess Maria Josepha, daughter of Empress Maria Theresa, was to marry King Ferdinand of Naples in Vienna. What a splendid chance to show off both his children! So on September 11, 1767, the Mozarts traveled to Vienna.

It was a terrible trip. An epidemic of smallpox broke out, and the wedding did not take place. The poor young archduchess came down with the disease and died on October 15. The Mozarts hurried to Olomouc in Moravia, but by then both Nannerl and Wolfgang had caught a mild case of the dreadful illness. A church official, who knew the family in Salzburg, took them in and saw that the children received the best medical care.

On December 23, everyone felt well enough to travel to Brno. There the prince-archbishop's brother invited them to stay with him for two weeks. Then, in January 1768, they returned to Vienna.

The widowed Maria Theresa welcomed the Mozarts back into her family circle. While she enjoyed talking with Anna Maria, her son, Joseph II—now the emperor—could entertain the rest of the family. But Maria Theresa had little heart for music these days. Not only was her husband dead, but now her daughter was gone too. Joseph wasn't interested either. He didn't want to spend money on music. So the Mozarts faced some lean times.

Two other problems made their situation worse. Suddenly Wolfgang and Nannerl were too old to be wonder children anymore. No one could deny that, at sixteen, Nannerl had become a young lady. Wolfgang was hardly a grown man at twelve, but he wasn't a cute little boy either.

The second problem was more complicated. Wolfgang began to scare other musicians. Look how talented he is, they apparently thought. It won't be long until he is after our jobs. There is only one way to handle this. We'll pretend that he doesn't exist.

That is exactly what they did. "I find that all clavier players and composers in Vienna set themselves against our progress," raged Leopold. Only Georg Christoph Wagenseil (Maria Theresa's court composer and music master) showed them any kindness, he said, and Wagenseil had been too ill to do them much good.

At last, though, their luck seemed to change. Joseph II decided that Wolfgang should write an opera—and conduct it too. A comic opera would work best, thought the delighted Leopold. So Marco Coltellini, an Italian poet in Vienna, wrote a libretto[4] based on a comedy by Carlo Goldoni, and

4. A libretto is the text, the words of the story, for an opera.

Wolfgang wrote the music for *The Pretended Simpleton* (K. 51).

Once again, everything went wrong. First the singers liked their arias. Then they didn't. The orchestral players said they wouldn't play for a child conductor. Rumors flew through the air. Wolfgang didn't know Italian well enough to set it to music, said one. He didn't write the music at all, said another. His father did. Then the performers began rehearsing an entirely different opera.

". . . the whole hell of music is in revolt to prevent the world from witnessing a child's cleverness," Leopold wrote to Hagenauer. ". . . Believe me, I shall neglect nothing necessary to protect the honor of my child."

Fortunately, Wolfgang didn't have to spend all his time stuck in these grown-up intrigues. Dr. Franz Anton Mesmer[5] said he had a little theater in his garden and would love to have the boy write a short opera for him. So Wolfgang composed *Bastien and Bastienne* (K. 50), a charming little opera with a German text.

He also wrote two symphonies, two masses, a trumpet concerto, and an offertory anthem, "Veni sancte spiritus" ("Come, Holy Spirit," K. 47). One of the masses, the concerto, and the offertory were performed at the inauguration of a

5. A physician who later became famous for his discovery of healing by hypnotism, also called "mesmerism."

new chapel. Furthermore, Wolfgang conducted and everyone who was anyone came. That must have made the whole family feel better.

But the nonsense about *The Pretended Simpleton* dragged on and on. Nearly a year had passed and it was no closer to being performed than when Wolfgang had finished it. Finally the manager of the opera said he would do it under protest. But he would guarantee that the performers would play and sing as badly as possible.

Leopold told him to forget it, packed up the family, and headed back to Salzburg. They got home on January 5, 1769. What in the world would the prince-archbishop say this time? Leopold had been absent for over a year and had precious little to show for it. Maybe he didn't even have a job now.

But Prince-Archbishop Sigismund gave him the surprise of his life. He didn't rant or rave or scold or punish. Instead, he ordered that Wolfgang's opera be performed at his court and it was—on May 1.

Perhaps Leopold's heart was touched by that generous gesture. Or perhaps he was fed up with traveling. In any case, the family stayed home for almost a year. During that time, Wolfgang wrote religious works and instrumental pieces. Most of his works for orchestra were light, dancelike compositions, just right for Salzburg. And, at least for a while, Salzburg was just right for Wolfgang.

Chapter 5

A WARM WELCOME

"My heart is quite enraptured for pure joy, because I feel so merry on this journey, because it is so warm in our carriage, and because our coachman is a brave fellow who drives like the wind whenever the road at all permits it."

Anna Maria Mozart must have swallowed hard when she read those cheerful words from her son in December 1769. He was off again, this time to Italy, and only his father went with him.

Leopold had made careful plans for this journey. He knew it would be tremendously important for Wolfgang's career. The rest of the world would never take seriously any musician who had not studied in Italy. Furthermore, the Italians had to hear what Wolfgang, now almost fourteen, could do. Finally, the boy would learn, especially about opera, church music, and song.

Anna Maria knew all that. But she still must have felt a few qualms when she read about the brave, speedy driver.

Nannerl got a letter too. In it, Wolfgang teased her about a sleigh ride and a certain Herr von Mölk, whom she had left to "sigh and suffer so interminably." He also informed her that Herr Gellert, "the Leipzig poet, is dead and since his death has written no more poetry." No doubt she chuckled as she read her brother's nonsense. But she might have felt some pangs of regret too. After all, this was the first time she hadn't gone along. In the past, part of the fuss—and the glory—had been for her. Everyone said she performed just as well as Wolfgang and even he admitted that her compositions were good.

But Nannerl didn't show the same genius for composition that Wolfgang did. Besides, she was a girl. She would never receive commissions for great works or become music director at some nobleman's court. At the age of seventeen, no longer a child prodigy, she would not astonish the world with her playing. So she would be better off at home, turning her thoughts to marriage and a family of her own. Her auburn curls, blue eyes, and pretty shoulders guaranteed her plenty of suitors. But it would be a long time before Nannerl thought seriously about marriage.

Meanwhile, Wolfgang's happy romp through Italy continued. Once again, Leopold had armed himself with letters of introduction and recommendation. Some of the most valuable came from Johann Adolph Hasse, a famous old German composer who wrote Italian operas. This time the letters worked and the Italians welcomed Wolfgang and his father with open arms.

At Rovereto, the main church bulged with people waiting to hear Wolfgang play the organ. He could barely squeeze his way through to the instrument. The same thing happened at Verona, where he gave several other concerts besides. An artist painted his portrait, several poets wrote verses about him, and the bishop asked him to lunch. The visit to Mantua brought a huge concert and rave reviews. One man called him "a wonderwork of nature." A lady sent him a bouquet with a poem and four ducats (about $50) hidden in it.

". . . We are everywhere received with every imaginable courtesy," wrote Leopold to Anna Maria, "and are presented to the *haute noblesse* [high nobility] on all occasions."

By the end of January, the two Mozarts had reached Milan, where Wolfgang met the famous Italian composer Giovanni Battista Sammartini. Better yet, Wolfgang was asked to write an opera, *Mitridate, King of Ponto*. It would be performed the following Christmas.

But Wolfgang didn't spend every moment with concerts and compositions. It was carnival time in Milan and he dressed up in a fancy costume and enjoyed himself like everyone else. The Mozarts were staying at the Monastery of San Marco and the monks went out of their way to make them comfortable.

Perhaps Leopold did not enjoy himself quite as well, though, when he realized that they weren't earning much money on this journey.

"My sole satisfaction," he wrote to his wife, "is that we are regarded with considerable interest and appreciation here, and that the Italians recognize Wolfgang's talents."

That recognition must have felt very good indeed after the nastiness they had encountered in Vienna. Wolfgang was certainly in high spirits when he added a postscript to his father's letter to Mama and Nannerl:

". . . *Addio*, my children, farewell! I kiss Mama's hand a thousand times, and imprint a hundred little kisses or smacks on that wondrous horse-face of thine!"

At an inn in Lodi, he wrote his first string quartet (K. 80), and then it was on to Parma. There the Mozarts met an incredible woman, Lucrezia Agujari. She was the illegitimate child of an Italian nobleman, which could have been a problem for her if she had been a timid person. But Agujari, who had a remarkable voice, simply labeled herself "La Bastardella" and sang her way into the hearts of all who heard her. She could sing higher than anyone else Wolfgang had ever heard and he raved about her "gallant gullet."

By March 30 the travelers were in Florence. There Wolfgang made a new friend, an English boy his own age called Thomas Linley. Linley was a superb violinist and the two played duets and even gave a concert together. Their friendship was one of the magical kind that springs up at once, but lasts too. Unfortunately, the Mozarts had scheduled only a few days in Florence. Both Wolfgang and Linley cried when they had to part. They never met again. For a while they exchanged letters and Wolfgang always asked about his friend when he met someone from England. But when Thomas Linley was twenty-two, he drowned in a pond near London.

Leopold and Wolfgang made it to Rome in time for Holy Week. Like hordes of other tourists across the centuries, Wolfgang kissed the toe of the statue of Saint Peter. "But," he informed his mother and Nannerl, "because I have the misfortune to be so little, someone had to lift the under-signed old rascal, Wolfgang Mozart!"

He managed another triumph in Rome all by himself, though. For over a hundred years, the Papal Choir had per-formed a choral work, *Miserere*, by Gregorio Allegri in the Sistine Chapel during Holy Week. It was both beautiful and complicated and no one else was allowed to perform it or even copy the music. Anyone who dared might be excom-municated. Wolfgang listened carefully as the Papal Choir sang. Then he hurried back to his lodgings and wrote down the entire piece from memory.

Soon the whole city buzzed with the news. What would the pope do when he found out? Would he excommunicate Wolf-gang? Clement XIV did no such thing. In fact, upon their return to Rome a few months later, he honored Wolfgang with the Papal Order of the Golden Spur. This made the boy a *cavaliere,* a knight. But he didn't take the title all that seriously. He only used it when he wanted to please Papa or impress Nannerl with her little brother's importance.

Actually, Wolfgang's mind was filled with dozens of other things. There were arias to compose for his opera (*Mitridate*) due at Christmastime, and the arithmetic tables he had lost. Would Nannerl copy those tables again for him? At Naples he watched the volcano Vesuvius "smoking furiously" and marveled at the rough beggars. Apparently the king of Naples paid their chief a salary every month just to keep his rowdy crew in line.

"Pray let me know how Herr Canari does," he wrote Nannerl. "Does he still sing? Does he still whistle?"

Perhaps Wolfgang was feeling a little homesick by then. After Naples, he and his father headed back north. In Bologna, the Philharmonic Academy invited him to take the test for membership, even though their usual age limit was twenty. The test involved working out a difficult musical problem and Wolfgang did it in record time. The members of the academy unanimously elected him to membership.

This honor especially pleased Wolfgang because it made his teacher so happy. While in Bologna, Wolfgang was working with Padre Giovanni Battista Martini, a priest who was a famous composer and teacher, and a good friend to Wolfgang as well.

Month followed month, and around the middle of October, the Mozarts arrived back in Milan. Final work on Wolfgang's opera began and so did the professional jealousies and squabbles. But these seemed like nothing compared to the Viennese intrigues. The first performance of *Mitridate, King of Ponto* (K. 87) on December 26, 1770, conducted by Wolfgang from the harpsichord, was a great triumph. *Mitridate* was performed more than twenty times that season.

From Turin to Venice to Padua, Vicenza, and Verona the Mozarts traveled. Part of the time they relaxed, but Wolfgang also gave concerts and kept up a steady stream of compositions. Sometimes his fingers actually ached from so much writing.

At last, on March 28, 1771, the two exhausted travelers stumbled up the stairs at 9 Getreidegasse. They weren't much richer than they had been when they left home—at least not financially. But Wolfgang's mind was crammed with all he had learned and the cheers of the Italians still rang in his ears.

At Maria Theresa's court in Vienna

Chapter 6

THE CAGE

Empress Maria Theresa saw to it that Wolfgang didn't stay home long. Archduke Ferdinand, another of her children, planned to marry an Italian princess in Milan the following October. She had already arranged for the composer Johann Hasse to write an opera for the occasion. But she would like young Mozart to do a smaller piece, a *serenata*, for voices and instruments.

That little job could have turned into a monstrous headache for Wolfgang. First, he didn't even see the libretto until he and Leopold reached Milan on August 21. Second, his lodgings didn't exactly lend themselves to quiet thought.

"Above us is a violinist," he wrote Nannerl, "beneath us is another, next us is a singing-master who gives lessons, and in the last room opposite us is an oboe-player. That is jolly for composing. It gives one plenty of ideas."

But he plunged ahead happily and once again wrote until his fingers hurt. On October 17, the nobility greeted *Ascanio in Alba* (K. 111) with thunderous applause. In fact, they liked it better than Hasse's larger work. Maria Theresa was so pleased that she gave Wolfgang a diamond and gold watch with her picture on it.

But back in Salzburg, the Mozarts had some sad news. Prince-Archbishop Sigismund died on December 16. The old man had huffed and puffed a lot at Leopold's wandering ways. Still, on the whole he had been a kind employer who gave his people a good bit of freedom. His successor, Hieronymus Joseph Franz von Paula, Count of Colloredo, Prince-Bishop of Gurk, was named early in 1772. According to rumor, Colloredo could be tough.

Leopold decided to make a good impression right away. He talked the new archbishop into having Wolfgang write a serenata for his installation. Colloredo must have liked the work. At any rate, he gave sixteen-year-old Wolfgang a salary as *konzertmeister* (concert master), a job he had been doing for almost three years.

The archbishop also permitted Wolfgang and Leopold to travel once more to Milan in November of 1772. Wolfgang had been asked to write another opera, *Lucio Silla* (K. 135). In spite of the usual delays and changes, it did well too. In January of 1773, Wolfgang wrote a piece especially for one of the sopranos, the lovely *Exsultate, jubilate* (K. 165).

Meanwhile, poor Leopold had a painful bout of rheumatism. But that didn't stop him from limping around, trying to get Wolfgang a permanent job at Grand Duke Leopold's court in Florence. Unfortunately, he failed and around the middle of March, the Mozarts returned to Salzburg. None of them ever visited Italy again.

Folks in Salzburg had learned by then how life would be with their new archbishop. They didn't like it. Archbishop Colloredo was cold and haughty. He treated everyone like a servant and expected them to toe the line. That didn't set well with the fun-loving Salzburgers. It didn't set well with the Mozarts either. For months they stayed at home and behaved themselves. Then Leopold couldn't stand it anymore. He wrangled permission for himself and Wolfgang to travel to Vienna. Once there, he began spinning political webs in hopes of catching his son a job.

A position at the imperial court would be best. But neither Maria Theresa nor her son seemed interested. So Leopold turned to Giuseppe Bonno, the court composer, J.G. Noverre, the ballet master, their old friend Dr. Mesmer, and others. Nothing worked. In October, he and Wolfgang returned to Salzburg and the archbishop's iron hand.

It is hard to know exactly how Wolfgang felt during this period of his life, because he was with his family and didn't share his thoughts in letters. Surely he missed the adventures and triumphs of his visits to other countries. Salzburg must have seemed dull in comparison. Still, he did have his family who always knew how to have a good time together.

In the spring of 1773 they had moved into a larger apartment on the Hannibalplatz[1], which became the center of a lively social life. Wolfgang had friends with whom to play games and make music, and girls with whom to flirt. Above all, he loved composing. Masses and symphonies, concertos and chamber works flowed from his pen as 1773 melted into 1774. It was also his composing that gave him his next chance of escape.

Maximilian Joseph III, elector of Bavaria, commissioned Wolfgang to write a new comic opera, *The Pretended Garden-Girl* (K. 196), for the Munich carnival season of 1774-75. Although the chosen libretto was pretty silly, Wolfgang didn't care about that. Maximilian Joseph wanted the opera performed in Munich early in 1775 and he wanted Wolfgang there for the performance. Even Archbishop Colloredo couldn't say no to the elector. By early December, Wolfgang and Leopold were on their way.

In spite of a violent toothache the first few days, Wolfgang had a marvelous time during the carnival season. He looked at pretty girls and concluded that at least one back home was prettier. He went to a comedy and a masked ball. He swapped gossip and wrote to Mama and Nannerl. At the end of one letter, he sent "a thousand kisses to Bimperl," the family's pet dog. Yes, Wolfgang was happy again.

1. Today it is known as Marktplatz.

The first performance of his opera took place on January 13 and, much to his delight, Nannerl came to hear it. ". . . The whole theater was packed so full that many people were forced to turn away," he wrote his mother. "After each aria there was a terrible uproar with clapping and shouts of '*Viva Maestro.*' Her Highness the Electress and the Dowager . . . also called '*bravo*' to me."

Wolfgang and his father stayed on in Munich for two more performances of *The Pretended Garden-Girl*, one on February 3 and one on March 3. On the Sundays between, some of Wolfgang's religious compositions were performed in Munich churches. Maximilian Joseph liked these works very much and Leopold must have hoped the elector would offer Wolfgang a job at his court. But that didn't happen.

Once again it was back to Salzburg. Wolfgang tried to settle down to a quiet life. He wrote sonatas for violin and for organ and strings, the serenade in D major (K. 250) and the piano concerto in E-flat major (K. 271). But Archbishop Colloredo didn't really approve of these secular compositions. He wanted church music—period.

Wolfgang composed pieces for him, but more and more he felt trapped. His position at court was lowly and showed no signs of improving. His salary was a measly hundred and fifty gulden (about $750) a year, the same as that of a clerk. He had to get out of Salzburg, to find a place where he had a future. But how?

At last Leopold asked Archbishop Colloredo for permission to go on tour. The archbishop said no. So Leopold sent him a formal petition. All right, replied the archbishop, go where you like. You're both fired. Then he changed his mind again and told Leopold he could keep his job. But no tours.

Fine! thought Wolfgang. He was twenty-one. He would go alone.

Chapter 7

JOB HUNTING

Leopold didn't like that idea at all. Wolfgang was entirely too young to roam around Europe on his own. He would make a complete mess of the business side of touring. And he would probably get in trouble too—maybe even with girls.

Arguments must have buzzed like flies around the Mozart apartment for a while. But at last Leopold found a solution. Why couldn't Anna Maria go with Wolfgang? No reason at all!

Privately, Mama might have thought of several reasons, including the fact that she didn't *want* to go. Anna Maria was no longer a young woman and her roots had struck deep in the Salzburg soil. To tear herself away from her home and friends, husband and daughter, must have been one of the hardest things she ever had to do. But she did it.

September 23, 1777, was a dark day for the Mozarts. As the coach bearing Mama and Wolfgang lumbered off to

Munich, both Leopold and Nannerl went back to bed with heavy hearts. Poor little Bimperl the dog cuddled down next to Nannerl.

"Miss Bimpes too lives on in hope," Nannerl wrote to Wolfgang later, "for she stands or sits near the door for half-hours on end, thinking that every minute you are going to return."

Anna Maria rather liked Munich and said she wouldn't mind living there. But she sorely missed her family at home and detested traveling. In a letter to Leopold she wrote:

"I sweat so that the water runs down over my face from sheer pains with packing, may the deuce take travel, I feel as though I would push my feet in my mouth with weariness. I hope you and Nannerl may find yourselves well. . . . To Nannerl I sent a message, not to give Bimperl too much to eat . . ."

Of course Wolfgang realized all the sacrifices his family was making for him and did everything he could to find a job and support himself. From house to house he went, playing and charming with all his might. But by September 29, his spirits had already dropped.

"We have many good friends but most, unfortunately, able to do little or nothing for us," he wrote to Leopold. Prince Zeil told him that the elector had said he should go to Italy and make a name. "So there it is! Most of these great gentlemen have such a terrible mania for Italy!"

Another man, Herr Albert, suggested finding ten friends who would each contribute one ducat a month to Wolfgang's support. This would amount to one hundred twenty ducats (about $1,500) a year. While he lived on that money, Wolfgang could be building a reputation in Munich. In a year or two, perhaps the court would be begging him to take a position.

"How does this idea please Papa?" asked Wolfgang. "Is it not a friendly thought? Ought it not to be accepted if it is seriously proposed?"

Leopold didn't think so. In fact, he doubted if those ten generous people could be found. Better go on to another German court, he advised, preferably one not quite so much in love with Italian music. In a letter written on October 15, he got downright blunt.

"You have stayed too long in Munich," he said. "You must give one or two concerts in Augsburg and make some money, be it much or little. Fair words, eulogies, and *bravissimi* will pay neither postman nor landlord, and when there is nothing more to be made, one must move on at once."

By the seventeenth, Wolfgang was in Augsburg. Once again he sought out the town bigwigs and gave a concert as Papa had ordered. But he really wasn't impressed with musical life there. The only person he would miss when he left was his young cousin, Maria Anna Thekla.

Maria Anna, called Bäsle, was not especially pretty. But

she had a naughty streak that definitely appealed to Wolfgang. While visiting a monastery, they met a priest, a pompous fellow who had too much to drink and tried to flirt with Bäsle. Wolfgang promptly made up a risqué song about him and sang it to her under his breath. Later he wrote her some of the most suggestive letters he ever wrote to anyone—and Wolfgang was known for his spicy letters.

People have been shocked by this side of his personality. How could anyone who wrote such beautiful music come up with such coarse words and filthy jokes? What was the matter with him? Actually, Wolfgang wasn't very different from other folks in his part of the world then. Many Germanic people—and especially Salzburgers—loved to spice their talk with references to bodily functions. It was simply part of their sense of humor. All the Mozarts went along with the custom and snickered away at each other's cleverness. But Wolfgang and his mother seemed to enjoy it most.

From Augsburg, the two traveled on to a nobleman's country home at Hohenaltheim to see if perhaps a job waited for Wolfgang there. It didn't, so they continued to Mannheim and the court of the Elector Palatine Carl Theodor. He wasn't as big a fan of Italian music and composers as the other German aristocrats. He preferred French music. But he also tried to give German artists a chance. Leopold's hopes soared.

"I wish you could get something to do in Mannheim," he

wrote Wolfgang on November 1. "They constantly play German opera there. Perhaps you could get an order to compose one?"

At first it seemed as if Wolfgang's luck actually might turn. He became friends with several important musicians in Mannheim, including Christian Cannabich, a composer and conductor at court, Anton Raaff, a famous tenor, and Johann Baptist Wendling, a flute player and composer.

"The Elector, the lady, and the whole Court is very pleased with me," he wrote to Leopold.

But on November 28, he got a stern letter back. Papa, it seemed, felt he was doing a number of things wrong. Wolfgang tried to explain. It looked as if maybe—just *maybe*—the elector might invite him to spend the winter at Mannheim. "Ought I to leave now of all times," he pleaded, "when the most important step has been taken?"

In reply came another scolding letter in which Leopold warned him against trusting the wrong people and recommended having several plans of action at all times. Poor Wolfgang! He couldn't do anything right. And poor Leopold, fretting away in Salzburg, knew he should be out there managing his son's affairs.

By December 10, Wolfgang realized that he wouldn't be offered the job at court. For a while he toyed with the idea of going straight to Paris, perhaps with Wendling, the flutist, and an oboe player called Ramm. Anna Maria vetoed that plan. Wendling and Ramm were bad influences, she felt. Furthermore, she had no intention of plowing on to Paris in the dead of winter. No, they had better remain in Mannheim until spring. Wolfgang could earn enough to pay their room and board by giving lessons.

So 1778 began somewhat peacefully, if not profitably. At least Leopold's criticisms stopped for a while, although he couldn't resist passing on some paternal wisdom.

"You are but a young man, twenty-two years of age," he wrote on February 5. "Accordingly, you cannot have such settled gravity as would discourage any young fellow of whatever station in life—an adventurer, a roisterer—or any importer, old or young—from seeking your friendship and acquaintance to draw you into his company and then by degrees into his toils. One steps into them so unnoticeably and then can find no return. I will not even speak to you of women, for there the greatest reserve and prudence are necessary, Nature herself being our enemy."

Maybe Leopold had second sight. Or maybe he just understood his son. At any rate, he had barely sent that letter when he received one from Mannheim. Wolfgang was in love.

Chapter 8

LOVE AND TRAGEDY

The girl's name was Aloysia Weber and she was just sixteen. Christian Cannabich had introduced Wolfgang to her family. The father Fridolin, copied music, did a little singing, and was a prompter[1] at the opera. He didn't earn much, but, according to Wolfgang, "was a good honest German who brings up his children well." Mrs. Weber rented out rooms to supplement the family income.

Wolfgang felt sure the Webers' fortunes would change once the world took notice of the two older girls' fine soprano voices. Aloysia, he said, had "a pure and lovely voice. She only needs to study action, when she might be *prima donna* on any stage." He traveled with her and her father to Kirchheim where Aloysia performed his music for the princess of Weilberg.

---

1. A prompter assists by suggesting or saying the words when an opera singer falters or forgets lines.

They had no sooner returned when Wolfgang had a brilliant idea. He would go with the Webers—Fridolin, Aloysia, and Josefa, the oldest girl—to Italy. He would write operas, Aloysia would sing in them, and both would become famous. Meanwhile, Josefa could cook for all of them. Why, they would even be able to spend a couple of weeks in Salzburg on the way!

"This unfortunate family is so dear to me that my dearest wish would be to make them happy," he told Leopold.

Leopold exploded.

"My dear Son!" he wrote. "I have read your letter of the 4th with amazement and horror!" He was crushed. He could not sleep. Did Wolfgang want to end up "bedded on straw and penned in with an attic-full of starving children?" Take that girl to Italy as a *prima donna?* Ludicrous! "How can you have allowed yourself to be bewitched by such a monstrous idea even for an hour?" For page after page he raved on. "Off with you to Paris—and that soon!"

Wolfgang replied mildly. He suspected his father might disapprove. Actually he hadn't been all that serious about the idea himself "in our present circumstances." Perhaps Aloysia was a bit too young and needed to work on her acting.

In his next letter, Leopold scolded his son for not working hard enough. "You would rather, I suppose, leave your poor old father in need!" Wolfgang responded by telling him about an aria he had written for Aloysia. But he also said he would "endeavor to grow increasingly worthy of so good a father."

By March 7, he had completed his plans for travel to Paris and on March 14, he and Anna Maria set out. But Wolfgang left behind a promise to Aloysia. The moment he made his fortune in Paris, he would return to her.

Nine and a half days later, they reached the French capital. It didn't take Wolfgang long to see that he wouldn't make his fortune easily. First, all the musical circles were caught up in a huge argument. Did Gluck or Niccolò Piccinni write better operas? They spent so much time fighting that they had none to spare for listening to other music, including Wolfgang's.

Second, getting around in Paris was still close to impossible. Filth clogged the streets just as it had the last time the Mozarts were there and carriages cost money. Third, visits to aristocratic homes didn't seem to do much good anyway. People said hello, listened to Wolfgang play, told him he was astonishing, and then said good-bye.

"Altogether Paris is greatly changed," he wrote his father. "The French are not as polite as fifteen years ago. Their manners now border on coarseness and they are terribly discourteous."

The Duchesse de Chabot certainly didn't show him any courtesy. First she made him wait in a frigid room until his fingers were numb with cold. Then she gave him a "wretched, miserable pianoforte" to play on. Finally, to add insult to injury, she and her gentlemen friends would not stop sketching, "so that I had to play to the chairs, table, and walls." Fortunately the duke came in a bit later and gave Wolfgang his full attention. Then Wolfgang played his heart out, completely forgetting the cold, his headache, and all that had gone before.

After a while, he simply couldn't bring himself to call on the nobility anymore. This meant that he didn't get many private pupils. He didn't think much of those he had either. Why, the daughter of the Duc de Guines couldn't even write an original piece during her fourth lesson! ("Do you imagine everyone has your genius?" asked Leopold.)

Then a French horn player called Rudolph offered Wolfgang the position of court organist at Versailles. He would have to spend six months each year at the court, but could live where he wanted the rest of the time.

"You must not throw *that* away so lightly," wrote Leopold. But Wolfgang couldn't get excited about the job. He would be buried at Versailles, he figured. The salary wasn't all that great either, especially considering the cost of living in France. Eventually he turned down the offer.

The fact was that Wolfgang simply did not like France. He had come because Leopold insisted, but he didn't really want to be there. "I am tolerably well, thank God," he wrote on

May 29, "but my life often seems to be without rhyme or reason. I am neither hot nor cold—and take little joy in anything."

No doubt part of his problem was missing Aloysia. But he could have been depressed for another reason too. All his life he had obeyed his father and done everything he could to please him. But the time comes when every young person must start making independent decisions. Leopold himself had done that when he chose music over the priesthood. Now, perhaps, it was Wolfgang's turn to strike out on his own.

He couldn't, though, because Anna Maria was with him and he felt responsible for her. Not that she was a burden. She made friends, gazed at the sights, and wrote cheerful letters home. For three weeks in May she was ill, but seemed to recover and was soon praising the lovely summer weather. Only at the very end of a letter to Leopold on June 12 did she mention that her arm and eyes ached.

On June 19, Wolfgang came home to find her sick again. At first he tried giving her the household remedies his family had always used. They did no good. Soon she could barely hear or speak. The German doctor could do nothing for her and neither could the French one sent by their old friend Melchior Grimm. For two weeks Wolfgang, along with neighbors and friends, nursed her. Then, on July 3, 1778, she died.

That night, torn apart with grief himself, Wolfgang proved the sort of son and brother he really was. He simply could not tell Leopold and Nannerl that Anna Maria was dead. The shock would be too great for them. The last they had heard, she was feeling better. So he put aside his own feelings and wrote them a letter saying she was very ill. He spoke a great deal about God's will. To make the letter sound natural, he even talked about his work.

"My dear Mother is in the hands of the Almighty," he said near the end. "If He will grant her to be with us, as I pray He may, we will thank Him for his grace . . ."

Then he wrote a second letter, this one to an old family friend in Salzburg, Abbé Joseph Bullinger. He told Bullinger the truth. "Let me now beg you to do me one friendly service," he said, "to prepare my poor father very gently for this sad news. . . . I commend my poor sister to you also with all my heart. . . . Preserve my dear father and sister for me and pray send me a speedy answer."

At last, on July 9, he wrote again to Leopold. "On the evening of that same day, at twenty-one minutes past ten o'clock, my mother fell happily asleep in God." It was a long letter in which Wolfgang poured out his pains, his faith in God, and his deep love for his father and Nannerl. "We shall see her again and be more happily, more blissfully together than ever in this world."

Chapter 9

TRIALS AND A TRAP

No one knows which disease killed Anna Maria Mozart, although one doctor called it "internal inflammation." Wolfgang was simply relieved that she died peacefully. She had received the last rites of the Catholic church and was already in a coma when she slipped away. Friends helped him arrange for her burial at the Cemetery of Saint Eustache. Now all that remained for him to do was to get on with his life, to make his father and Nannerl proud of him.

His old friend Melchior Grimm, now a baron, invited Wolfgang to live with him for a while. It seemed a good idea at first. Wolfgang had a pleasant room and could set about his business as he liked. But it didn't work out.

Part of the problem was that he just didn't have enough business in Paris. His debts kept mounting and he had to borrow money from Grimm. At least once the baron wrote to Leopold in despair. "I wish that, for his own good, he had half the talent and twice the ability to handle people."

But Wolfgang didn't want to handle the people who needed handling in Paris. He despised them. He wrote one of his great symphonies during this period, the symphony in D major (K. 297). But, "whether it will please, I do not know!" he told Leopold. "And to tell the truth, I care very little. . . . I guarantee that it will please the *few* intelligent French people present; as for the stupid ones—I see no great misfortune in its not pleasing them." Later in the same letter, he called his French audience "asses" and "oxen."

In spite of all this, the symphony was a tremendous success and is still called the Paris symphony. But the time had come for Wolfgang to leave and everyone knew it. Baron Grimm dropped some very heavy hints and even offered to pay Wolfgang's coach fare home. But it was Leopold, as usual, who got his son moving.

Both the organist and the music director at Salzburg had died and the court was in an uproar. If Wolfgang came back to fill the organist's post, Leopold could become music director. Furthermore, Wolfgang might travel whenever he wanted to write operas and he would receive a decent salary.

None of this appealed to Wolfgang in the least. He didn't want to live in pokey Salzburg with grim old Archbishop Colloredo as his boss. But Leopold kept putting on the pressure. It just so happened, he said, that the court needed another soprano. Maybe Aloysia could get the job. Then he appealed to Wolfgang's sympathy.

"You will scarcely know your poor father. . . . I was ill when you left a year ago—and what have I not had to go through in this year? I have a constitution of iron or I should be dead already; only if you will not lift this black burden from my heart by your presence it will crush me utterly. . . . You alone can save me from death . . ."

Wolfgang gave in. He accepted Grimm's offer of coach fare too, although he later raged when he found out that the baron had chosen the slowest, cheapest coach for him. On September 26, 1778, he left Paris for Nancy and, after a break there, went on to Strasbourg. A few concerts in Strasbourg earned him a little money and he decided to stop by Mannheim next.

That decision gave Leopold some anxious moments. What if the foolish young man ended up staying in Mannheim? Sure enough, Wolfgang heard rumors that he might be appointed opera conductor at the National Theater. "In a word," he told Leopold, "Mannheim loves me as I love Mannheim."

"Really I know not what I should write," replied Leopold. "I shall go mad or die of a decline."

He didn't have to do either. The Bavarian Elector Maximilian III had died, and Elector Palatine Carl Theodor had moved his whole court—including the Webers—to Munich to take over. By Christmas Day, Wolfgang was there, and so was his cousin Bäsle. "Perhaps you may find you have a great part to play," Wolfgang had written her. Did he picture her as bridesmaid at his wedding? No one is quite sure.

But at long last he saw his Aloysia again. What a fine young lady she had become—so tall, so confident! Her life had changed a great deal. Her career had begun to soar and the elector himself took a special interest in her. She now earned over twice as much as her father. Surely, though, she would remember the poor young composer who had been willing to give up everything for her. She remembered—and she made fun of his clothes.

The story goes that Wolfgang laughed, sat down at a clavier, and sang a little song. "I gladly leave that maiden that will not have me." Some say the song continued with coarse words of his own invention. In any case, the romance had ended and by mid-January 1779, Wolfgang was back in Salzburg.

His family welcomed him home with kisses and roast capons. But in no time Wolfgang felt trapped again. Although he was now the court organist, he thought the archbishop was an overbearing tyrant, and the archbishop thought he was a conceited young brat. For almost two years they ground along together and neither changed his opinion of the other.

As usual, Wolfgang took refuge in his composing. He wrote masses and symphonies, sonatas, concertos, and chamber music. But what he really wanted to write was opera and Salzburg had no permanent opera company. That made him feel even more trapped.

Then, in 1780, Carl Theodor invited him to write an opera for the next carnival season in Munich. Wolfgang was overjoyed. Once again Archbishop Colloredo had to say yes, since the elector had made the request. At least for a short time, Wolfgang would be free—and writing opera. In addition, his old friend Wendling's wife and daughter would sing two of the parts in the new opera and Anton Raaff would sing a third.

By early November, Wolfgang had arrived in Munich to work with the singers on *Idomeneo, King of Crete* (K. 366). Even they seemed more cooperative than in the past. Leopold must have received his son's cheerful letters with mixed feelings. Of course he was pleased that things were going so well. But he missed being part of the excitement himself. He also missed Wolfgang—and worried about him.

"Should you fall sick (which God forbid!)," he wrote, "do not conceal it from me so that I can come at once and take care of you."

All that troubled Wolfgang, though, was a cold and the fig juice and oil of almonds Leopold had already recommended seemed to be helping that. A flood of compliments from the musicians after the first rehearsal of *Idomeneo* helped too.

On January 29, 1781, the performance took place. Leopold had cleverly waited until the archbishop left for Vienna,

67

then grabbed his hat and Nannerl and rushed to Munich to see it. None of the Mozarts hurried back to Salzburg either. They would be home soon enough. They might as well enjoy the carnival while they could.

When they did return, Archbishop Colloredo decided to show them again who was boss. He ordered Wolfgang to join him in Vienna at once. Wolfgang went. Then the archbishop said he must stay with the rest of the servants. This meant Wolfgang couldn't perform in various homes and earn a little extra money. Furthermore, he must eat with the servants. For the time being, he obeyed. But his temper began to simmer.

Soon he found that some of the nobility wanted him to dine with them. He did it. Archbishop Colloredo ordered him to show up at the Russian ambassador's house as a servant. He went as a guest and the ambassador welcomed him warmly. Furious, the archbishop said Wolfgang could not perform at a benefit concert for the widows of musicians. Wolfgang performed. Very well, growled Archbishop Colloredo, Wolfgang could not give a public concert of his own.

Obviously this could not go on much longer. One day the archbishop called Wolfgang a scoundrel, a lousy rascal, and the most slovenly fellow he knew—to his face. He suggested that he would be better off without Wolfgang's services. Wolfgang resigned. He had to submit that resignation in writing three times before it was accepted. Then one of Colloredo's courtiers literally kicked him out of the house.

For a while, Wolfgang swore that he would kick that courtier back. Then he gave up the idea. Why bother? He had what he wanted now. He was free of the archbishop for good. In fact, for the very first time in his life, Wolfgang was on his own.

Mozart's birthplace

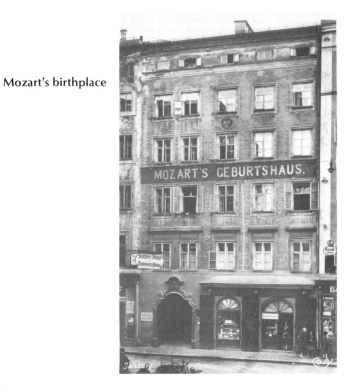

Salzburg, the home of the Mozart family

Maria Anna (Nannerl), 1762

Wolfgang, 1756

Wolfgang and Nannerl performing

A copy of Mozart's
first composition

Mozart at age
eleven

Above: Franz Joseph Haydn and Constanze Mozart
Below: Beethoven playing for Mozart

Above: A performance of *Abduction from the Seraglio* in 1854 in London

Below: A recent performance of *Così fan tutte*

Although very ill,
Mozart worked on the
Requiem.

A stone marking
Mozart's grave was put
up in 1859.

Mozart wearing his decoration as Knight of the Golden Spur

Chapter 10

BEGINNINGS

Leopold was anxious. Would the fuming archbishop now fire Leopold too? Good heavens, they might all starve!

But Wolfgang didn't worry. He had friends in Vienna and he would soon have plenty of work. If Archbishop Colloredo bore a grudge against Leopold, Papa and Nannerl could just pack up and come live with him.

Fortunately, the archbishop had calmed down by the time he got back to Salzburg. At least he didn't take his anger out on Leopold. It would have been interesting, though, to see Wolfgang's family in his new lodgings. He had moved in with some friends—the Webers.

This family had come to Vienna when Aloysia was offered a singing engagement there. Fridolin died almost at once and Mrs. Weber, Maria Cäcilie, hoped her talented older daughters would support the family. But it didn't work out that way. Even Wolfgang was disgusted with his former sweetheart's behavior.

"This girl hung round her parents' neck before she was able to earn money," he wrote. "No sooner had the time come when she could show herself beholden to her parents . . . than she left her poor mother, flung herself at a comedian,[1] married him—and her mother has not that much from her."

So Aloysia was gone and Josefa couldn't find work. Constanze, age eighteen, had a good voice too, but wasn't ready for professional jobs. Sophie, the youngest, was still a child. That left Maria Cäcilie to keep the family going and she did it by opening her home to lodgers. Naturally she was delighted when Wolfgang showed up.

Naturally Leopold was *not* delighted. None of his letters after January 1781 have survived, but Wolfgang's replies make their contents clear.

"I do not know how to begin this letter, my dearest father," he wrote on May 19, "for I cannot recover from my astonishment, and never shall be able to do so if you continue to think and write as you do."

Apparently Leopold had written, among other things, that he could not believe Wolfgang was right to resign. In fact, the only way to save his honor, said Papa, was to withdraw that resignation.

"Impossible!" said Wolfgang.

---

1. Actually, Joseph Lang, Aloysia's husband, acted in tragedies. The marriage turned out badly.

Back and forth flew the letters. But this time Wolfgang was determined to make it on his own. He gave some lessons, although most of the rich Viennese had moved to their country homes for the summer. He published six sonatas for piano and violin (K. 296 and 376-80). Best of all, he got to work on a new opera.

Empress Maria Theresa had died in November 1780 and her son, Joseph II, now ruled alone. Joseph decided to set up a national opera company that would appeal to ordinary people as well as educated music lovers. This company would put on a form of comic opera called *Singspiel* (sing-play). The characters spoke much of the story—in German. But they also sang. To Wolfgang's great joy, Joseph invited him to write one of the operas.

An actor called Gottlieb Stephanie wrote the libretto for *The Abduction from the Seraglio*[2] (K. 384), a story set in Turkey. Then Wolfgang got busy with the music.

"I hasten to my desk with the greatest eagerness," he told Leopold, "and sit there in the most absolute content."

Meanwhile, much to his annoyance, he had to find someplace else to live. Folks in Vienna had begun to gossip about him and Constanze Weber.

"I live with them, therefore I am to marry the daughter!" he complained to Leopold on July 25. ". . . If ever in my life I

2. A seraglio is a harem.

have put aside all thoughts of marriage, it is just now! . . . I am just beginning to live, and am I to poison my life for myself? . . . I play and joke with her when time permits . . . and—that is all! If I had to marry all the ladies with whom I have jested, I should have two hundred wives at least!"

He found a new room, but informed Leopold that it was "fit for rats and mice." So he looked for another. At the same time, he ran into a problem with one of his students, Josepha von Avernhammer. This young lady had already told him that she would never marry. She planned to earn her living as a concert pianist. According to a letter from Wolfgang to Leopold on August 22, she must have changed her mind.

"She is as fat as a farm wench, sweats in a way to make one sick, and goes so scantily clad that one can read as plain as print: 'Pray, look here!' True, to look is enough to strike one blind. . . . She is seriously in love with me! I thought it a joke, but I know it is true."

In spite of all his ranting, Wolfgang wasn't opposed to the idea of marriage. When he learned that Nannerl had been ill, he wrote and suggested that "the best cure for you would be a husband . . ." By December 15, he felt that the best cure for him would be a wife. Only as a married man could he live a happy, moral life. He hoped Leopold wouldn't be horrified, but the person he wanted to marry was Constanze Weber.

"She is not ugly, but no one could call her a beauty. Her

whole beauty consists in two little black eyes and a graceful figure. She has no wit, but wholesome common sense enough to fulfill her duties as wife and mother. She is *not* inclined to extravagance. . . . She dresses her own hair every day—understands housekeeping, has the kindest heart in the world, and—I love her and she me with all our hearts!"

Constanze's life at home was not easy, he said. Her older sisters always got the better of everything while she had to do all the work. Still, he knew he couldn't afford to marry her yet. He must have some sort of steady income first.

By December 22, he had more news for Leopold. The gossip about him and Constanze had reached her guardian, Johann von Thorwart. Thorwart gave Wolfgang an ultimatum. He could sign a marriage contract or he could stop seeing Constanze. If he signed the contract, he must marry her within three years or else pay her a yearly sum of three hundred florins (about $750) for the rest of her life. Wolfgang signed. But the moment her guardian left, Constanze asked her mother for the contract.

"Dear Mozart!" she said. "I need no written assurance from you. I trust your word—thus!" And she tore up the contract.

"I had no fear but that you would give your consent to the marriage when the right time came," continued Wolfgang's letter, ". . . God grant I may be able to marry her soon!"

We can only imagine Leopold's reaction.

While all this was going on, Emperor Joseph had his troubles too. Some distinguished visitors from Russia had been staying with him and he was running out of ways to keep them amused. Why not hold a contest, he thought, between Wolfgang and the talented young Italian composer-pianist Muzio Clementi? This event took place on December 24. Both musicians played their own works, sight-read those of others, and improvised. Joseph felt that Wolfgang won. Clementi had played with art, but Wolfgang with both art and taste. For a while, Wolfgang even thought Joseph might offer him a job at court. But he didn't. He already had a court composer, the Italian Antonio Salieri, and didn't think he needed another.

Still, 1782 began as a good year for Wolfgang. He had recently met the composer Franz Joseph Haydn, whose music he had known and liked for years. Now he became friends with the older man. They didn't see one another very often because Haydn spent most of his time at his patron's country estate. But they kept in touch when they could.

Wolfgang also found a few more pupils and played a couple of concerts. Then, on July 16, 1782, his *Abduction from the Seraglio* was performed. Vienna loved it. People wanted to hear it again and again and every performance was sold out. Wolfgang didn't even mind when the emperor told him he had put too many notes in the opera. He simply replied that he had used exactly as many as he needed.

During this period, he tried to spend time with Constanze too, although he didn't particularly enjoy his visits to her home. Maria Cäcilie had always drunk too much and now she had become just plain mean. For a while, Constanze moved out and stayed with a friend. But her mother threatened to send the police after her, so she returned home again. Maria Cäcilie felt sure that the young couple would live with her and pay room and board after they got married. Neither had the nerve to tell her how wrong she was.

At the same time, Constanze tried to make friends with Wolfgang's family. She wrote a pathetic little letter to Nannerl because "your Brother assured me that you would not be offended." She also added a postscript to one of Wolfgang's letters to his father. Nannerl's reply was not unkind, although she never really liked Constanze. But, according to Wolfgang, all Leopold sent was advice. Wolfgang felt it was too late for that. He loved Constanze and must marry her.

The young couple did have one quarrel. Constanze had been playing the game of forfeits at a party and failed to answer one of the questions correctly. As her forfeit, she had to let a young man measure the calves of her legs with a ribbon. Wolfgang was appalled. Any self-respecting woman would have taken the ribbon and measured her calves herself, he scolded. In fact, as a "promised bride," she shouldn't have been playing the game in the first place.

Constanze, equally furious, told Wolfgang that she didn't

want to have any more to do with him. Soon, though, she was his "dear Constanze" again.

During July, he quickly composed a serenade for the Haffner family back in Salzburg. It later became his symphony in D major (K. 385), known as the Haffner symphony. He also wrote a serenade in C minor for wind instruments (K. 388). But he couldn't get Constanze and her unhappy home life out of his mind. He had asked his father again and again for permission to marry. Finally he couldn't wait any more.

On August 4, 1782, Wolfgang Amadeus Mozart, age twenty-six, and Constanze Weber, age twenty, were wed. Leopold's permission arrived the next day.

Chapter 11

FAMILY LIFE

Five guests attended the Mozart wedding—Constanze's mother and youngest sister, Sophie, her guardian, von Thorwart, her friend Herr von Zetto, and Wolfgang's friend, Gilofsky. According to Wolfgang, both he and Constanze cried, which made everyone else, including the priest, cry too. In the evening, another friend, the Baroness von Waldstädten, held a supper for the newlyweds. It was, Wolfgang told his father, *princely*.

The festivities had barely ended when he began to drop hints about taking Constanze to Salzburg for a visit. He loved his father and sister and adored his new wife. If they could all learn to care for one another, life would be perfect.

At the same time, he took a long, hard look at his career. He wanted to stay in Vienna. But as he wrote Leopold, "these Viennese gentry (by which I chiefly mean the Emperor) must not imagine that I am in the world purely for the sake of Vienna!" He preferred to work for Joseph II, but would not beg him for a job. Perhaps he should try Paris again, or even England. He had already taken three lessons in English, just in case.

These vague plans made Leopold so nervous that he wrote to Baroness von Waldstädten. Wolfgang *mustn't* go running off across Europe. Sooner or later a post would open for him at the Viennese court. All he needed was a little patience.

Wolfgang didn't find it too difficult to take his father's advice. He had a number of students now and some friends among the nobility who cared about his work. On Sunday mornings he played at musicals in the home of Baron Gottfried van Swieten. He also set up concerts of his own.

Arranging concerts took a lot of work, though. He had to choose a good date, find and rent a hall, hire orchestral musicians, send out publicity, arrange for tickets, sell them, write the music, and then play or conduct it. A typical concert took place in March 1783. It included the Haffner symphony, an aria, a piano concerto, a scene from an opera, a little symphony, another concerto, another scene from an opera, two sets of variations, another aria, and a movement from a symphony. Joseph II came to this concert and sent Wolfgang twenty-five ducats (a little over $300).

Near the end of 1782, Wolfgang composed three new piano concertos (K. 413-15). This form of music let him show off his playing as well as his composing. Besides, audiences seemed to like them.

Meanwhile, he and Constanze took life one day at a time. Sometimes they had plenty of money. Then they lived in a nice apartment. When the cash ran out, they moved someplace shabbier. Through good times and bad, Wolfgang usually managed to have someone come in to do his hair each morning. He felt that a musician in his position must look prosperous even when he wasn't. He also charmed Baroness von Walstädten into giving him a "beautiful red coat" with mother-of-pearl buttons.

"I should like to have all my things of good quality, workmanship, and appearance!" he told her.

When his finances were especially shaky, he borrowed money from her and other friends.

"In Heaven's name," he wrote to her in February 1783, "I beg your Ladyship help me to save my good name and my honor!"

But during this same period, he and Constanze managed to enjoy the carnival season in Vienna. Wolfgang borrowed his father's harlequin costume to wear to the masquerades and the young couple even gave a ball of their own.

In early May, Wolfgang wrote Leopold from the Prater, a park in Vienna, where they had gone for an all-day picnic. Constanze would soon be having their first child and her "fat and flourishing husband" felt that a day outdoors in the beautiful weather would do her good.

He wrote his father again on June 18.

"I congratulate you, you are a grandpapa! Early yesterday morning, the 17th, at half-past six, my dear wife was happily delivered of a fine, big, sturdy, fat boy!"

They named the child Raimund Leopold. Wolfgang had firm ideas about how he should be raised. Constanze must not nurse him. Actually, a diet of sugar water would be best for the infant. After all, it had done wonders for him and Nannerl. But friends warned him that people in Vienna did not know how to use sugar water properly. So he gave in and hired a wet nurse.

By the end of July, he felt that he and Constanze could safely leave little Raimund and make their long-postponed trip to Salzburg. It would have been natural for them to ask Constanze's mother to baby-sit while they were gone. Even though they hadn't seen much of her since their marriage, she had helped with the child's birth and looked after Constanze while she recovered. But for some reason (perhaps Maria Cäcilie's drinking problem), they chose to board Raimund at a home for babies.

Wolfgang had great hopes for this visit home. Most of all, he wanted his father and sister to welcome Constanze with open arms. They might even give her some trinket to show that she was now truly part of the family. But he had a project in mind too. Before their marriage, Constanze had been very ill. If she recovered and became his wife, he had vowed, he would write a mass in thanksgiving. The time had come to finish that mass, so he took it with him. Perhaps it could even be performed in Salzburg.

Unfortunately, the warm welcome did not take place. Leopold and Nannerl were polite to Constanze, but that was all. Both she and Wolfgang felt hurt and disappointed. At least, though, they had the mass to think about. On October 25, Wolfgang's Mass in C minor (K. 427) was performed at Saint Peter's in Salzburg. Constanze herself sang the difficult soprano part.

Neither she nor Wolfgang must have known then that six days earlier, on August 19, their baby had died. He was just two months and two days old. According to the death certificate, he died of dysentery. Many people lost infants and young children to such diseases in those days. But that didn't make the pain any easier to bear. Wolfgang and Constanze must have found it difficult to go on with their visit in the chilly atmosphere of the Mozart home.

Maybe they could see no reason to hurry back to Vienna now that Raimund was gone. At any rate, they stayed in Salzburg until late October. While they were there, Wolfgang did a favor for his friend Michael Haydn, younger brother of Franz Joseph.

Michael, who worked for the archbishop, was supposed to write two sonatas for violin and viola. But he was sick or indisposed. So Wolfgang wrote the sonatas for him and submitted them as Michael's work. The archbishop accepted them quite happily, never dreaming that they were really by "the most slovenly fellow he knew."

On their way back to Vienna, Wolfgang and Constanze stopped at Linz, where they stayed with Count Thun, the father of one of Wolfgang's pupils. Could Wolfgang, wondered the count, write him a symphony for a private concert on November 4? That gave Wolfgang no more than a few days. He was, of course, able to do it. Furthermore, the Linz symphony (K. 425) is still considered one of his finest.

For the rest of 1783 and on into 1784, he continued to compose. He wrote fantasies for the piano, a quintet for horn and strings, a horn concerto, a string quartet, a violin sonata, and various vocal works. In spite of the sad visit to Salzburg, he also went on writing his father faithfully and filled his letters with details of his work and family life. On May 26, he told Leopold about the problems he and Constanze were having with their maid. Apparently the girl did very little work, drank a great deal of beer, and then had the gall to complain about her employers.

August brought good news from Salzburg. At the age of thirty-three, Nannerl had decided to get married. She and her husband, Baron Berchtold von Sonnenburg, would live at Saint Gilgen, not far from Salzburg, in the house where Nannerl's mother had been born. The baron, a widower, already had five children when he married Nannerl and she soon gave him three more.

"My wife and I wish you all happiness and joy in your change of state," wrote Wolfgang to his sister, "and only regret most sincerely that we cannot have the pleasure of being present at your wedding."

They had good reason to avoid rough journeys at the time. Constanze was pregnant again. On September 21, 1784, she gave birth to their second son, Karl Thomas. This time the baby lived.

Mozart, 1878

Chapter 12

FRIENDS

Soon after Karl's birth, Wolfgang decided to move his family again. They did so much entertaining and now with a baby to think about—well, they simply needed more room. The apartment he found was at 846 Schulerstrasse. The rent was a little more, but he knew he would find the money somewhere.

He certainly had no trouble digging up thirty-four kreuzer (about $2.50) to buy himself a pet starling. This clever bird could whistle the melody Wolfgang used in the last movement of his piano concerto in G major (K. 453).

A new group of British friends spent much time with the young Mozarts during this period. Stephen Storace was a composer and violinist who wanted to study with Wolfgang. His younger sister, Nancy, sang with the opera. Thomas Attwood, an organist, studied with Wolfgang too and Michael Kelly, a tenor from Ireland, completed the circle.

Years later, Kelly wrote about the first time he met the

Mozarts. The evening began with a private concert at which Wolfgang "favored the company by performing fantasies and capriccios on the pianoforte." To Kelly's delight, he sat between the Mozarts at dinner. As always, Wolfgang talked to him about Thomas Linley, his English friend from long ago.

After dinner came dancing, in which Wolfgang enthusiastically joined. Constanze told Kelly that she sometimes thought her husband really preferred dancing to music.

"He was a remarkably small man," continued Kelly, "very thin and pale, with a profusion of fine hair of which he was rather vain."

After that first evening, Kelly got to know the Mozarts much better. He spent hours playing billiards at their apartment, where Wolfgang had an excellent table. "Many and many a game have I played with him," confessed Kelly, "but always came off second best." He also noticed that Wolfgang was "remarkably fond of punch, of which beverage I have seen him take copious draughts."

Then there were the Sunday concerts, which Kelly wouldn't miss for the world. Wolfgang was "kindhearted and always ready to oblige," wrote Kelly, "but so very particular when he played that, if the slightest noise were made, he instantly left off."

No doubt Wolfgang enjoyed these British friends even more because he remembered his own happy stay in England as a child. Now and then he still thought about visiting that country again and he loved to practice his English. One note he gave Attwood said, "This after noon I am not at home, therefore I pray you to come to morrow at three & a half. Mozart."

Another special friend turned up in Vienna late in 1784. Franz Joseph Haydn had come with his patron, Prince Nicholas Esterházy, for a long stay at the prince's winter home. There were musical evenings and Haydn invited Wolfgang to play at some of them. In return, Wolfgang asked Haydn to his home to play string quartets. Haydn himself played first violin at these gatherings. Other friends played second violin and cello, while Wolfgang chose the viola. He said he liked sitting in the middle with the music all around him.

Seeing Haydn again gave him an idea. Why not dedicate a set of six string quartets to his friend? Haydn had practically invented the form. What better tribute could Wolfgang give him? Fortunately, he had already written three. He finished up the others by January 14, then wrote a dedication to go with his gift.

"I send my six sons to you, most celebrated and dear friend. . . . Please receive them kindly and be to them a father, guide, and friend."

In February Leopold arrived in Vienna for a long visit. One Friday evening, Haydn and two friends came over to play through the three new quartets. Sometime during the evening, Haydn took Leopold aside. "I tell you," he said, "calling God to witness and speaking as a man of honor, that your son is the greatest composer I know, either personally or by repute! He has taste, and, in addition, the most complete understanding of composition." The buttons must have popped right off Leopold's coat.

Nor could he contain his pride when he heard Wolfgang's piano concerto in G (K. 453). "Tears came to my eyes for sheer delight," he wrote Nannerl. Furthermore, the emperor waved his hat and called out, "Bravo, Mozart!"

Wolfgang also introduced his father to some new ideas during his visit. For quite a while, the young composer had been interested in Freemasonry. This movement intrigued many people in Vienna at that time with its emphasis on brotherhood and high ideals. Wolfgang also enjoyed the contact it gave him with all sorts of people. He joined a lodge of Freemasons and persuaded Leopold to become a member too. Neither man gave up his Catholic faith. They just added Freemasonry to their system of beliefs.

Yes, thought Leopold, Wolfgang was doing very well. He was earning money now and Constanze seemed to manage her home as a dutiful and thrifty wife should. Soon the pair of them ought to have a healthy little sum put away in the bank. Wolfgang never told him how quickly the money melted away.

As 1785 marched on, an idea he had tucked away in the back of his mind began to stir and buzz until it gave him no peace. Back in 1784, he had met the Italian composer, Giovanni Paisiello. Paisiello had composed an opera called *The Barber of Seville*, based on a comedy by the French writer Beaumarchais. *The Barber* by Beaumarchais had a sequel, Wolfgang knew, called *The Marriage of Figaro*. It would make a magnificent opera. Much to his disgust, German opera had lost favor again in Vienna. Probably he should be thinking about doing a work in the Italian style himself.

But *Figaro* had its problems. First of all, Wolfgang would need a fine librettist to work out the text. Second, the story contained a lot of political ideas of which the emperor disapproved. The solution to both these problems turned out to be a poet called Lorenzo Da Ponte.

Da Ponte's own life story could have made a colorful opera. Born an Orthodox Jew, he had been ordained a Catholic priest, but moved to Venice and spent most of his time gambling and with women. Eventually, he had to leave town and settled in Vienna instead. His career as a poet, he felt, might do better if he could find the right composers with whom to work. Wolfgang seemed a good choice and also had a terrific story in mind—*Figaro*.

We will do it, decided Da Ponte. Don't worry about the political bits. I'll just tell the emperor that I took them all out.

So both men got busy and found that they worked together beautifully. Not that *Figaro* didn't run into more difficulties. As usual, the Italians at court, probably led by Salieri, fought against it. But at least the singers liked the music. Among them were two of Wolfgang's dear friends, Nancy Storace and Michael Kelly.

On May 1, 1786, the first performance of *The Marriage of Figaro* (K. 492) took place. The audience wanted so many numbers repeated that it lasted almost twice as long as it should have. But it didn't make Wolfgang's fortune.

He had been paid a lump sum at the beginning. Debts and other expenses soon chewed that away. Then the Spanish composer, Vincente Martín y Soler, presented an opera to which the fickle audiences flocked. *Figaro* played only nine times between May and December. Then it was withdrawn.

Meanwhile, Wolfgang faced more heartbreak in his personal life too. On October 18, 1786, Constanze had another child, Johann Thomas Leopold. On November 15, the baby died. Once again the family had to pull their shattered lives together and go on. Wolfgang did it the only way he knew. He wrote more music.

Chapter 13

THE PRAGUE CONNECTION

Sometime during Johann Thomas's short life, Wolfgang began to dream again of traveling to England. But he couldn't bear to leave Constanze behind and she couldn't travel with two babies. At last he thought of a solution. He would send the children to Salzburg with two servant girls and Leopold could look after them.

Leopold disagreed vehemently. "I have had today to answer a letter of your brother's which has cost me a great deal of writing," he said in a letter to Nannerl on November 17. ". . . He made no less a proposition than that *I* should take charge of his two children as he wished to make a tour through Germany and England, etc., at mid-Lent! . . . A pretty suggestion indeed! They are to set out light-heartedly on their travels, die perhaps, perhaps stay in England—in which case I could come running after them with the children and so on! . . . My refusal is a forcible one—and instructive, too, if he will but profit by the lesson!"

By the time Wolfgang received that refusal, his infant son had died. Maybe Leopold would have made his words less "forcible," if he had known.

Soon, though, the Mozarts had another chance to travel. Pasquale Bondini, an impresario,[1] had arranged for performances of *The Marriage of Figaro* in Prague. Why shouldn't Wolfgang go and see how folks in the Bohemian capital liked his opera? Besides, the change of scene would do Constanze good after all she had been through. So early in January 1787, they set off.

The next month must have been one of the happiest they had known in a long time. They stayed with Count Johann Joseph Thun and had other friends, including Franz and Josepha Dusek, around them. *Figaro* had already been performed and, according to Wolfgang, "Here they talk of nothing but *Figaro;* scrape, blow, sing, and whistle nothing but *Figaro;* visit no opera but *Figaro*, and eternally *Figaro*." Even when attending a ball, they found that many of the melodies for the dances had been taken from *Figaro*.

On January 17, they went to see Prague's *Figaro* themselves. In no time, the whole audience knew that Mozart was there. The moment the overture ended, they roared their approval. On the nineteenth, Wolfgang gave them the first performance of a symphony he had written just a month

1. A promoter or manager of an opera or concert company

before. From then on, the symphony in D major (K. 504) has been known as the Prague. On the twentieth, he delighted his enthusiastic fans still further by conducting *Figaro* himself.

We must bring him back to Prague, thought his friends, the Dusceks. Pasquale Bondini agreed. Wolfgang left the friendly city a hundred ducats (about $1,250) richer. He was to return in the fall with a new opera written especially for Prague.

Lorenzo Da Ponte knew the perfect subject for that new opera—Don Juan. This story of an unscrupulous seducer had been set to music before, both as an opera and as a ballet. But Da Ponte felt that no one could do it as well as he and Wolfgang could. He probably also chuckled at the idea of writing about a hero so much like himself.

About this time, Wolfgang's British friends, the Storaces, Attwood, and Kelly, all went back to England. Part of him longed to go with them, but it just wasn't possible then. Instead, they promised to see if they could find a position for him. If so, he could join them later.

Meanwhile, composition again filled his mind. He wrote two string quintets, a violin sonata, and the serenade for strings, *Eine kleine Nachtmusik* (*A Little Night Music*, K. 525). Of course he had his opera, *Don Giovanni*,[2] too. But he

2. Italian for Don Juan

did take some time off to meet a seventeen-year-old boy who wanted to play the piano for him. Wolfgang was quite impressed with the talent of that young boy, whose name was Ludwig van Beethoven.

On April 4, he wrote a touching letter to his father. "But now I hear you are really ill! I am sure I need not tell you how greatly I long for reassuring news from yourself." He begged Leopold to let him know if he didn't get better, "so that I can come with all human speed to your arms!" Then he ended the letter with a thousand kisses from himself, Constanze, and Karl.

Leopold Mozart died on May 28, 1787. He was sixty-eight years old. Wolfgang received the news the next day and wept bitterly. Leopold had not been an easy father. His constant advice and meddling would have driven many young people to harsh words and open rebellion. But Wolfgang never stopped loving him and never broke the bond of close communication between them.

About a week after Leopold's death, Wolfgang's pet starling died. He had grown very fond of that bird and decided to give it a full-fledged funeral, complete with music, in his garden. It began "Here lies a cherished fool, a starling bird."

By October 1, he and Constanze were on the road to Prague again, part of *Don Giovanni* with them. Wolfgang would write the rest when he got there. He often worked that way. When he was feeling good, he once told a friend, musical ideas simply flowed through his mind. He remembered those he liked best and began to figure out how he might use them. "All this fires my soul," he said and eventually he could imagine a whole work, not as it would be played, note after note, but all at once, in one glance, "All this inventing, this producing," he said, "takes place in a pleasing, lively dream." He remembered the whole work too until he had a chance to write it down. The writing itself took time, but wasn't hard.

No doubt Wolfgang composed the remaining sections of *Don Giovanni* that way. One story says that the musicians got the music to the overture so late that they had to sight-read it at the performance. But Constanze said that Wolfgang finished it the night before the dress rehearsal and she should have known. She was the one who had to keep him awake with punch and stories as he wrote.

Actually, the first performance didn't take place as early as planned. Singers in Prague weren't quite as professional as those in Vienna and needed more help learning their parts. They also kept getting sick. While they struggled, the usual backstage stories flew thick and fast. One told about the soprano who wouldn't scream as she was supposed to offstage. Wolfgang grabbed her from behind and she gave exactly the yell he wanted.

Other stories maintained that he had affairs with most of the women in the cast. There is absolutely no proof that these stories were true. Wolfgang could flirt all right, but chances are that he remained faithful to Constanze throughout their marriage.

Finally, on October 29, 1787, *Don Giovanni* (K. 527) had its first performance in Prague. The city went mad. They loved it and Wolfgang couldn't help loving them in return.

He and Constanze had been dividing their time between an inn and the Duseks' country home. Now the Duseks urged them to stay longer. Why hurry home? They were having so much fun. Constanze, who was pregnant again, seemed to be feeling fine. So they did stay a little longer.

One day Josepha Dusek locked Wolfgang up in a summerhouse. She wouldn't let him out, she said, until he wrote the concert aria he had promised her. All right, said Wolfgang. But she couldn't have it unless she was able to sight-read it perfectly. He purposely made it as hard as he could. But that didn't bother Josepha, who was an excellent musician. She sang the aria beautifully and Wolfgang immediately dedicated it to her.

The Mozarts didn't return to Vienna until mid-November. They had no idea what new problems they might have to face there. But they had brought back with them hearts full of happy memories of Prague, one city that truly appreciated Wolfgang's genius.

Chapter 14

DEBTS AND DEPRESSION

No one knows exactly why the Mozarts had so many money problems. There were probably several reasons. Wolfgang was never a practical person. When he had money, he liked to spend it. Constanze seemed thriftier, but she was easygoing too. She would never deny her Wolfgang anything he wanted. Besides, she was pregnant and often ill. Managing the family's helter-skelter finances might have been simply too much for her.

Another clue to the mystery turned up toward the end of 1787. Wolfgang and Constanze had barely returned from Prague when Christoph Willibald Gluck, a famous composer and chamber musician to the court, died. Joseph II gave Wolfgang the job. Gluck's salary, though, had been two thousand gulden (about $10,000) a year. Wolfgang would receive only eight hundred gulden (about $4,000). That wasn't the only time someone underpaid him for his work. But it is one of the most obvious times.

The new job meant that Wolfgang had to write dances for the balls at court and he plunged at once into a set of three (K. 534-36). Constanze also had a new offering to make. On December 27, she gave birth to their first daughter, Theresia.

On May 7, 1788, Viennese audiences had their first chance to hear *Don Giovanni*. "So what?" they responded. Even the emperor knew better than that. "The opera is divine, perhaps even more beautiful than *Figaro*," he told Da Ponte, "but no food for the teeth of my Viennese."

So Wolfgang gave them more of what they wanted—dances. By this time he was so poor that he moved his family to a home in the country outside Vienna. There he didn't have to pay quite so much rent, but still his debts grew. In June he turned in despair to his friend and lodge brother, Michael Puchberg.

"If you would be so kind, so friendly, as to lend me the sum of one or two thousand gulden [$5,000 or $10,000] for a period of one or two years, at a suitable interest, you would be doing me a most radical service!"

This was the first of many times that Wolfgang appealed to Puchberg, and his friend almost always came through. Sometimes Puchberg must have felt certain that he would never see his money again. But eventually he did get it back, plus the dedication of one of Wolfgang's most lovely chamber works, the divertimento in E-flat for string trio (K. 563).

The composer borrowed from other friends too, including

Franz Hofdemel. From Hofdemel he asked only one hundred gulden (about $500). Life plays strange tricks, though. In 1970, Wolfgang's letter requesting that loan sold at an auction in Germany for $5,738.

Wolfgang also tried to repair his ailing fortunes by writing more symphonies. Between June and mid-August 1788, he composed three, the E-flat major (K. 543), the G minor (K. 550), and the C major, known as the Jupiter (K. 551). These were the last symphonies he ever wrote and, many feel, the greatest. But tragedy interrupted his work on them too. On June 29, 1788, his baby daughter, Theresia, died.

By fall, Wolfgang's old friend, Baron van Swieten, had stepped in with financial help. He planned to give private performances of some of Handel's oratorios, but would not have an organ available on which to play the accompaniments. Would Wolfgang write different accompaniments for him? Of course.

In the spring of 1789, Wolfgang had a different chance to earn money, a trip to Germany with Prince Karl Lichnowsky. True, he didn't know how much he would earn. But travel always raised his spirits, so on April 8, he and the prince set out in the prince's private coach. They visited Prague, Dresden, Leipzig, Potsdam, and Berlin. Wolfgang did manage to make a little money here and there. But one of the greatest treasures he found on this journey had nothing to do with finances.

At Saint Thomas's Church in Leipzig, he was invited to play the same organ that Johann Sebastian Bach had played for more than twenty-five years. Then the choir performed Bach's motet, "Singet dem Herrn" ("Sing to the Lord"), for Wolfgang. Wolfgang was stunned. "Here, for once, is something from which one may learn!" he cried. He immediately asked for some of Bach's other motets.

By the time he reached home again on June 4, he had no more money than when he had left. "As regards my return, you will have to look forward to me more than to the money," he had warned Constanze. But he did have commissions to write six string quartets and six piano sonatas.

For the first time, though, events in his personal life cast such a heavy shadow that he couldn't work. Constanze was pregnant again—and ill. She absolutely must go to the spa at Baden. But there was no money to send her. Wolfgang couldn't bear it. Paralyzed with depression, he wrote to Puchberg.

"My God, I could not wish my worst enemy in my present case! And if you, my best friend and brother, forsake me, I, unfortunate and blameless, and my poor sick wife and child, are all lost together!"

This time he wanted only five hundred florins (about $1,250) and promised to pay them back at a rate of ten florins per month. Puchberg came through and Constanze went to Baden.

By the end of August, Wolfgang was composing again. *Figaro* was to be put on and one of the sopranos wanted more arias. He also wrote a piano sonata and the quintet for clarinet and strings (K. 581). Most exciting of all, he had been asked to compose a new opera, *Così fan tutte*[1] (K. 588), with Da Ponte. While he was working on that, Constanze had her child, a girl named Anna Maria. This baby lived only an hour.

On January 26, 1790, Vienna heard—and liked—the new opera. Unfortunately, Joseph II died on February 20 and the whole country went into mourning. Performances of *Così* had to be shelved until June when life returned to normal again.

In March, Leopold II became emperor and Salieri resigned as music director. Wolfgang's heart must have leaped. Might he get Salieri's job at last? He didn't. Leopold chose Joseph Weigl instead. Then might Wolfgang become *second* music director, write church music, teach the royal children? No. Leopold flatly ignored him. Later, when the king of Naples visited, the emperor treated him to operas by Weigl and Salieri. He didn't include even one of Wolfgang's.

A deep depression settled over the Mozarts then. By June, Constanze was back at Baden where she had to take the

---

1. Così fan tutte is an Italian phrase that cannot really be translated. "Girls will be girls" is about as close an English version as is possible.

baths sixty times. Soon Wolfgang became ill too and financial difficulties mounted. There must be *something* Wolfgang could do. But for the moment, he couldn't see what.

Chapter 15

"LACRYMOSA"

When the answer finally came to him, he recognized it as an old familiar one. He must travel. The new emperor's official coronation would take place in Frankfurt on October 9. The court planned to take many musicians along for the ceremonies, but not Wolfgang. Very well, he thought. He would go unofficially with his brother-in-law, Franz Hofer, Josefa's husband. He would have to pawn the family silver to pay his expenses. But with all the musical hullabaloo going on, he should find plenty of chances to make some money.

The two men left on September 23 and had a pleasant journey. "My carriage (I should like to give it a kiss!) is magnificent," Wolfgang wrote to Constanze. He played concerts in Frankfurt and other cities and even got to perform for the king of Naples after all, at the elector of Bavaria's court. But when he returned home in November, his pockets were as empty as they had ever been.

So he fell back on his two standard methods. He borrowed

money and wrote more music. From his pen flowed two string quintets, three pieces for mechanical organ, still more dances, and his last piano concerto (in B-flat major, K. 595). The manager of an opera company in England invited him to come there and write operas, and Haydn's impresario, Johann Peter Salomon, said he would soon feature Wolfgang's works on his London concerts. But Wolfgang didn't go. Maybe he just couldn't afford the trip. Or maybe his last illness had already taken hold of him.

He perked up, though, when Emanuel Schikaneder came to him with an idea. Schikaneder wasn't the most honest man in the world, but he knew a lot about the theater. He had been putting on all sorts of performances at the Theater auf der Wieden on the outskirts of Vienna. Now he wanted to do a "magic opera," complete with fantasy, comedy, exotic costumes and settings, animals, and plenty of stage effects. He wanted Wolfgang to compose the music.

Wolfgang had his doubts. He had never written a "magic opera" before. But Schikaneder presented him with a libretto he had put together himself from bits and pieces of plays he liked and Wolfgang got to work. To make sure he kept on working, Schikaneder set him up in a little summerhouse near the theater. Wolfgang had always liked composing outdoors, so that was fine with him. Besides, whenever Schikaneder saw him getting weary, he took him out for a few drinks.

Wolfgang pinned his hopes on that new opera. Once again Constanze, pregnant and ill, had to pack up little Karl and go to Baden. Wolfgang missed her dreadfully and wrote her almost every day.

"Hold your hands up in the air—" he said in a letter on June 6, "2999½ little kisses are flying from me to you and waiting to be snapped up."

He also went to see her whenever he could. On June 18 at Baden, he wrote the incredibly beautiful motet, "Ave verum corpus" (K. 618). Then it was back to Vienna and more work.

By July he had almost finished the new opera and Schikaneder had begun rehearsals. Then, out of the blue, came two new commissions. The first had all the trappings of a ghost story and gave birth to many legends and rumors in the years that followed. One day a mysterious stranger appeared at Wolfgang's door and asked him to write a requiem, a funeral mass. He would be well paid for his work. But he must never tell anyone he had done it.

Who was this stranger? Was it Salieri, playing a fiendish trick? Was it death himself, come for Wolfgang? The answer wasn't nearly so dramatic. A certain nobleman of that time, Count Franz von Walsegg-Stuppach, liked to play at being a composer. But he did not have a speck of talent. So he paid other composers to write anonymous works, then had them performed at private concerts and told everyone he had written them himself. His wife had died earlier that year, which is why he wanted a requiem. It was his servant who had come rapping at Wolfgang's door.

But Wolfgang himself didn't know that. Ill, depressed, and lonely for Constanze, he too began to wonder whether he wasn't writing the funeral mass for himself. Fortunately, Constanze gave birth to her sixth child, Franz Xaver Wolfgang, on July 26 and soon felt well enough to return to her husband. By that time, he was up to his ears in the second commission.

Leopold still had to be crowned king of Bohemia and Wolfgang's faithful friends in Prague wanted him to write an opera for the occasion. Unfortunately, they gave him very little notice. They also chose a libretto, *La clemenza di Tito* (*The Generosity of Titus*), which was dry as dust. But Wolfgang couldn't say no to them.

Swaying and bouncing along in the coach to Prague, Constanze at his side, he composed in his head. Each night, he sat down at an inn and wrote out the day's thoughts. His pupil, Franz Süssmayr, got to do the recitatives[1]. All in all, Wolfgang finished the opera (K. 621) in eighteen days. On September 6, it received its first performance. It was not a big hit, but it wasn't a flop either.

That frantic pace of work did not do Wolfgang's health

---

1. A rhythmic free vocal style that is not speaking, but not singing either.

any good. By the middle of September, he knew that he was seriously ill. Still, he managed to write a clarinet concerto (K. 622) for his friend Anton Stadler, and to conduct the first two performances of the opera he had written with Schikaneder.

Many people believe that *The Magic Flute* (K. 620) is one of the greatest operas ever written. Vienna didn't grasp that right away. The whole thing was so *strange*, full of symbols and mystery, a bit like a fairy tale, but not quite. Soon, though, *The Magic Flute* cast its spell on them. It was performed twenty-four times in October alone. Even Salieri and his mistress came to hear it and sat in Wolfgang's box with him.

"You cannot imagine how pleasant they were and how much they liked not only my music but the libretto and everything," he wrote to Constanze, who was back at Baden.

With *Tito* and *Flute* successfully launched, he could get back to work on the *Requiem* (K. 626). But his health grew worse and worse. His hands and feet swelled, he vomited and had terrible headaches, and sometimes he even fainted. During one period, he began to think that someone was poisoning him and some of his symptoms did point to poison. But they also pointed to chronic kidney disease, which most scholars now think he had. Later, rumors sprang up that Salieri had poisoned him. These stories haunted the old Italian composer until he died. But neither Wolfgang nor his family ever accused him of such a thing. In fact, Wolfgang's son Franz Xaver later studied with Salieri.

When Constanze came home, she urged her husband to rest. But he couldn't stay away from that *Requiem*. For a short period in November, he felt better and wrote the *Little Masonic Cantata* (K. 623). By the end of the month, though, he had to stay in bed, nursed by Constanze and her sister Sophie.

Each evening, music from *The Magic Flute* filled his mind and he held his watch so he would know just where the performers were. But he could no longer bear the singing of his current Herr Canari and sadly asked his nurses to have the little bird moved to another room. In spite of everything, the *Requiem* still fascinated him. He talked to Franz Süssmayr about his ideas for it and asked Süssmayr and other friends to sing it with him. On December 4, they had just started the "Lacrymosa" ("Weeping") section when Wolfgang began to cry and they stopped. Soon he was partially paralyzed. A priest came to give him the last rites and he said good-bye to his family. But a moment later, he opened his mouth again and tried to sing part of the *Requiem*.

Near midnight, Wolfgang seemed at peace, and at 12:55 A.M. on December 5, 1791, he died. He was thirty-five years old.

Chapter 16

AFTERWARDS

Details about Wolfgang's funeral have never been clear. It took place either on December 6 or 7. The weather was either snowy, rainy, or mild with mist. The religious ceremony was held either at an indoor or an outdoor chapel. Baron van Swieten either talked Constanze into giving her husband a third-class funeral, which cost about thirty dollars, or made the arrangements himself.

We do know that no one went all the way to Saint Mark's Cemetery with Wolfgang's body, which was placed with others in a common grave. We don't know exactly where that grave is. Almost a hundred years later, music critic George Bernard Shaw said that Wolfgang probably wasn't buried at all. He just shook his bones into the grave and "soared off into universality." Shaw may have been right.

But Wolfgang did have at least one splendid memorial service. On December 14, Prague, the city that honored him while he was alive, marked his death with both a service and a concert at Saint Nicholas's Church. Three thousand mourners crowded into the building. Two thousand more shed their tears in the bitter cold outside.

For a while after Wolfgang's death, Constanze was too shattered by grief to do much of anything. But then she pulled herself together, asked Süssmayr to complete the *Requiem*, and got busy settling the family's debts and finding an income for their future. She organized concerts of Wolfgang's music and, like her mother, rented out rooms. One of her lodgers, Georg Nikolaus von Nissen, eventually became her second husband. Constanze lived to be seventy-nine and spent the last years of her life in Salzburg.

One of her neighbors was Nannerl, who had moved back to Salzburg with her children in 1801 when her husband died. There she gave piano lessons. Later years were not so kind to Nannerl, she went blind and became almost deaf, and had very little money. She died in 1829 at the age of seventy-eight. Nannerl and Constanze never did become friends.

Wolfgang's sons, Karl Thomas and Franz Xaver, both grew up and tried to find careers in music. Karl Thomas did not do well and ended up as a staff official for the viceroy of Naples. But Franz Xaver became a concert pianist, conductor, and composer. His works are rarely performed now, but were popular during his lifetime. Neither son married nor had children, so Wolfgang has no direct descendents today.

Franz Joseph Haydn lived until 1809. He was terribly upset to hear about Wolfgang's death and tried to get English publishers to bring out his works. "He stood far above me," said Haydn. When the old man died, Vienna's musicians came together to honor him at his funeral. The music they played was Wolfgang's *Requiem*.

Wolfgang Amadeus Mozart 1756-1791

1756 Wolfgang Amadeus Mozart is born on January 27. George Frideric Handel writes his oratorio, *The Triumph of Time and Truth*. The French drive Britain from the Great Lakes in the North American colonies. Cotton velvets are first made in England. The first chocolate factory is established in Germany. Frederick II, the Great, starts Seven Years' War by attacking Saxony.

1757 The first public concert is held in Philadelphia. The Royal Library in London is transferred to the British Museum.

1758 George Washington and John Forbes take Fort Duquesne, later renamed Pittsburgh. The first English manual on guitar playing is published. A canal is begun between Liverpool and Leeds in Great Britain.

1759 British gain Quebec, in the American colonies, from the French. Franz Joseph Haydn composes his first symphony. Handel dies.

1760 The Russians occupy and burn Berlin, Germany. King George II of England dies and is succeeded by George III. The first exhibition of contemporary art is held at the Royal Society of Arts, London. Josiah Wedgwood founds pottery works at Staffordshire, England.

1761 Mozart writes his first composition, a minuet. Christoph Willibald Gluck writes his ballet *Don Juan*. The first French veterinary school is established in Lyon. London opens the first exhibit of agricultural machines.

1762 Mozart and his sister, Nannerl, begin tours as musical prodigies. Gluck's opera, *Orpheus and Euridice*, is performed in Vienna. A Russo-Prussian alliance against Austria is signed. Catherine II, the Great, becomes empress of Russia. In Scotland, cast iron is converted for the first time into malleable iron.

1763 The Peace of Paris ends the Seven Years' War. In the American colonies, the rising of the Indians near Detroit spreads east; a British proclamation provides government for Quebec, Florida, and Grenada. The German botanist Josef Kolreuter fertilizes plants by animal carriers of pollen.

1764 Mozart writes his first symphony. James Watt invents the condenser, the first step toward the steam engine. London introduces the practice of numbering houses.

1765 The British Parliament passes the Stamp Act for taxing the American colonies. The potato becomes the most important European foodstuff. The Bank of Prussia is founded by Frederick the Great. Canning by hermetic sealing is introduced.

1766 After a journey of over three years, the Mozart family returns to Salzburg. The Stamp Act is repealed, but the Declaratory Act affirms Britain's right to tax the colonies. The first paved sidewalk is laid in Westminster, England. Henry Cavendish discovers that hydrogen is less dense than air.

1767 The Mozart family leaves for Vienna. Emperor Joseph II asks Mozart to compose and conduct an opera, which is *The Pretended Simpleton*. Taxes are placed on imports of tea, glass, paper, and dyestuffs in the American colonies.

1768 Mozart composes *Bastien et Bastienne* for Dr. Franz Anton Mesmer. Boston citizens in the colonies refuse to quarter British troops. The Royal Academy in London is founded. The first numbers of the weekly *Encyclopaedia Britannica* are published. Captain James Cook makes his first sea journey around the world.

1769 Mozart goes to Italy with his father. He receives honorary (without a salary) appointment as concertmaster to archbishop of Salzburg. Privy Council in London decides to retain tea duty in American colonies. The future emperor Napoleon I is born in Corsica.

1770 Mozart writes his opera, *Mitridate, King of Ponto* and its first performance is a success. In Italy Mozart meets and becomes friends with fourteen-year-old English violinist Thomas Linley. Mozart begins taking lessons from Padre Martini. The Philharmonic Academy of Bologna unanimously elects Mozart as a member. In Rome he is named *cavaliere* of the Papal Order of the Golden Spur. Handel's *Messiah* is performed in New York. Freemasons of Germany founded in Berlin. Ludwig van Beethoven is born. The Boston Massacre takes place. The British Parliament repeals duties on paper, dyestuffs, and glass in the American colonies, but keeps tax on tea. Civil liberties, international free trade, textile machines, and steam power lead England to an industrial revolution that spreads round the world.

1771 Mozart and his father return to Salzburg. *Ascanio in Alba* premieres in Milan. Mozart and his father begin their second Italian journey. The first edition of the *Encyclopaedia Britannica* is published.

1772 Colloredo becomes prince-archbishop of Salzburg. Mozart is named konzertmeister, and receives a salary. *Lucio Silla* is performed in Milan. The Boston Assembly demands rights of colonies and threatens secession. Samuel Adams forms Committees of Correspondence in Massachusetts for action against Great Britain. The first carriage traffic crosses Brenner Pass between Austria and Italy.

1773 *Exsultate, jubilate* is performed in Milan. The Boston Tea Party protests the tax on tea. The waltz becomes popular in Vienna.

1774 The Virginia House of Burgesses decides to call the Continental Congress. It meets in Philadelphia with representatives of all colonies except Georgia. Rules are drawn up for the game of cricket.

1775 *The Pretended Garden-Girl* is performed in Munich. Beaumarchais's opera, *The Barber of Seville*, is premiered. The American Revolution begins. Paul Revere rides from Charleston to Lexington. The Second Continental Congress assembles at Philadelphia. George Washington becomes commander-in-chief of the American forces.

1776 The American Congress carries the Declaration of Independence.

1777 Mozart begins Paris journey with his mother. The British are defeated at Princeton, New Jersey and Bennington, Vermont. The Stars and Stripes are adopted as the flag of the Continental Congress.

1778 Mozart writes a ballet in Paris, *Les Petits Riens*. Paris symphony performed to great success. Mozart's mother dies in Paris on July 3. La Scala in Milan and the National Singspiel in Vienna open. The American colonies sign treaties with France and Holland. Ludwig van Beethoven (at age eight) is presented by his father as a six-year-old prodigy. The first children's clinic opens in Paris.

1780 Haydn composes the Toy symphony. Maria Theresa dies, succeeded by Joseph II. The first Sunday newspapers appear in London. The circular saw is invented.

1781 Mozart's opera *Idomeneo, King of Crete* is presented in Munich. The British capitulate at Yorktown and evacuate Charleston and Savannah in the North American colonies.

1782 Mozart's opera, *The Abduction from the Seraglio*, is presented in Vienna. He marries Constanze Weber. Mozart composes the Haffner symphony. Johann Christian Bach dies. Spain completes the conquest of Florida in North America. The Montgolfier brothers construct an air balloon. James Watt invents the double-acting steam engine.

121

1783 Mozart's first child, Raimund Leopold, is born June 17 and dies August 19. Mozart and Constanze visit Salzburg. Johann Adolph Hasse dies. Great Britain recognizes the independence of the United States. Beethoven's first works are printed. Mozart completes the Mass in C Minor. The first paddle-wheel steamboat is sailed on the Saone River.

1784 Nannerl marries Baron Berchtold von Sonnenburg. Mozart's second child, Karl Thomas, is born on September 21. Mozart is accepted into the Freemason lodge. Mozart begins collaboration with Lorenzo Da Ponte. Thomas Rowlandson produces the first political cartoons. A Swiss inventor designs an oil burner. English mathematician George Atwood accurately determines the acceleration of a free-falling body. The first balloon ascent takes place in England. The first school for the blind is founded in Paris.

1785 Mozart composes six "Haydn" string quartets. Jean-Pierre-Francois Blanchard and John Jeffries cross the English Channel in a balloon.

1786 Mozart's *Marriage of Figaro* is presented in Vienna. Mozart's third child, Johann Thomas Leopold, is born on October 18 and dies November 15. The earliest attempts are made to install gas lighting in Germany and England.

1787 Mozart's *Figaro* is presented in Prague and is a success. Mozart writes *Eine Kleine Nachtmusik* and *Don Giovanni* premieres in Prague. Leopold Mozart dies in Salzburg at age sixty-eight on May 28. Mozart's fourth child, Theresia, is born on December 27. Gluck dies. A constitutional convention convenes in Philadelphia. A steamboat is launched on the Delaware River. Dollar currency is introduced in the United States.

1788 Theresia dies on June 29. *Don Giovanni* is received unenthusiastically in Vienna. Mozart composes three great symphonies: E-flat major, G minor, and the Jupiter. Carl Philipp Emanuel Bach dies. New York is declared the capital of the United States.

1789 Constanze makes her first of many visits to a spa in Baden. Their fifth child, Anna Maria, is born on November 16 and dies one hour later. The first United States Congress meets in New York. George Washington is inaugurated as president, John Adams vice-president. A revolution takes place in France. The first steam-driven cotton factory is built in Manchester, England.

1790 Mozart's opera, *Così fan tutte*, is presented in Vienna. Constanze again in Baden. Joseph II dies. Washington, D.C., is founded.

1791 Mozart plays his piano concerto (K. 595). Franz Xaver Wolfgang, Mozart's sixth child, is born on July 26. Mozart conducts the festival performance of *Don Giovanni* in Prague. *La clemenze di Tito* premieres in Prague with Mozart conducting. Constanze goes to the spa in Baden. *The Magic Flute* is performed in Vienna. Mozart dies on December 5. The first ten amendments to the United States constitution (Bill of Rights) are ratified. The waltz becomes fashionable in England.

INDEX- *Page numbers in boldface type indicate illustrations.*

Abduction from the Seraglio, **74**, 79, 82
Agujari, Lucrezia, 40
Aix-la-Chapelle, 24
Albert, Herr, 53
Allegri, Gregorio, 41
Amalia, Princess (Prussia), 24
Archduke Ferdinand, 45
arias, 26, 42, 59
Ascanio in Alba, 45-46
Attwood, Thomas, 93, 95, 101
Augsburg, 22, 53, 54
Avernhammer, Josepha von, 80
"Ave verum corpus," 113
Bach, Johann Christian, 27-28
Bach, Johann Sebastian, 27, 108
Baden, 108-110, 115
ballets, 18
Baratier, Jean-Philippe, 15, 16
Bäsle. (*See* Thekla, Maria Anna)
Bastien and Bastienne, 35
Bavaria, 16
Beaumarchais, 97
Beethoven, Ludwig van, **73**, 102
Berlin, 24, 107
Bimperl (family dog), 48, 52
Bologna, 42
Bondini, Pasquale, 100, 101
Bonno, Giuseppe, 47
Brno, 33
Brussels, 24
Bullinger, Abbé Joseph, 62
Canari, Herr (family pet), 11, 42
cantata, 32
Cannabich, Christian, 55, 57
Canterbury Cathedral, 28
Carl Theodor, Elector Palatine, 54, 65, 67
Caroline, Princess (Holland), 28, 29
Chabot, Duchesse de, 59-60
chamber music, 18, 48, 66
Charlotte, Queen (England), 26
chorus, 28
clavecin, 23

clavier lessons/playing, 12-13, 32
Clementi, Muzio, 82
Clement XIV, 41-42
Colloredo, Archbishop (Hieronymus Joseph
   Franz von Paula), 46, 47, 48, 50, 64, 67,
   68, 77
Coltellini, Marco, 34
"Come, Holy Spirit," 35
compositions, 13, 28, 32, 35-36, 39, 40, 43,
   45-46, 48-49, 64, 67, 79, 84, 86, 89, 90, 93,
   96, 98, 101, 104, 106, 107, 109, 112, 113-116
concertos, 13-14, 32, 35, 48, 66, 90, 115
Così fan tutte, **74**, 109
counterpoint, 32
Danube River, 17
Da Ponte, Lorenzo, 97, 101, 106, 109
Don Giovanni, 101, 102, 103, 104, 106
Dresden, 107
Dusek, Franz, 100, 101, 104
Dusek, Josepha, 100, 101, 104
Eine kleine Nachtmusik, 101
England, 27, 28
Esterházy, Prince Nicholas, 95
Eugen, Duke Carl, 22
Exsultate, jubilate, 46
Ferdinand, King (Naples), 33
Florence, 40, 41, 47
Francis I (Holy Roman Emperor), 19
Frankfurt, 23, 111
Freemasonry, 96
French Revolution, 19
Gellert, Herr, 38
George III (England), 26, 27
Gilofsky, 85
Gluck, Christoph Willibald, 59, 105
Goethe, Johann Wolfgang, 23-24
Goldoni, Carlo, 34
Grimm, Friedrich Melchior, 25, 61, 63,
   65
Guines, Duc de, 60
Haffner family, 84
Haffner symphony, 84, 86

Hagenauer, Lorenz, 23, 26, 35
Handel, George Frideric, 26
harpsichord, 23
Hasse, Johann Adolph, 38, 45, 46
Haydn, Franz Joseph, 19, **73**, 82, 89, 95-96, 112, 119
Haydn, Michael, 89
Heinecken, Christian Heinrich, 15
Hofdemel, Franz, 107
Hofer, Franz, 111
Hofer, Josefa, 111
Hohenaltheim, 54
Hohensalzburg, 9
Holland, 28-29
Idomeneo, King of Crete, 67
Ips, monastery of, 17
Italian music, 18-19
Italian tour, 37-38
Joseph II, 33-34, 79, 82, 85-86, 105, 109
Kelly, Michael, 93, 94, 98, 101
Kinsky, Countess, 20
Kirchheim, 57
konzertmeister, 46
La clemenza di Tito, 114
"Lacrymosa" section, 116
Lang, Joseph, 78
Leipzig, 107, 108
Leopold, Grand Duke, 47
Leopold II, 109
libretto, 34
Lichnowsky, Prince Karl, 107
Linley, Thomas, 40-41, 94
Linz, 17, 90
Little Masonic Cantata, 116
Little Night Music, 101
Lodi, 40
London, 26, 27
London, Tower of, 28
Louis XV (France), 25
Lucio Silla, 46
Ludwigsburg, 22
Magic Flute, 115, 116

Mannheim, 54-56, 65
Maria Antoinette, 19
Maria Josepha, Archduchess, 33, 34
Maria Theresa, 19, 25, 33, **44**, 45, 46, 47, 79
Marriage of Figaro, 97, 98, 100, 101, 106, 109
Martini, Padre Giovanni Battista, 42-43
masses, 35, 48, 66, 89
Maximilian Joseph III, elector of Bavaria, 17, 48, 49, 65
Mesmer, Franz Anton, 35, 47
mesmerism, 35
Milan, 39, 43, 45, 46
minuets, 13, 18
Miserere, 41
Mitridate, King of Ponto, 39, 42, 43
Mölk, Herr von, 38
Moravia, 33
Motet, 108
Mozart, Anna Maria (daughter), 109
Mozart, Anna Maria Pertl (mother), 9, 11, 20, 33, 37-40, 48, 51-52, 59, 61, 63
Mozart, Constanze Weber (wife), **73**, 78-81, 83-85, 87-91, 96, 98-99, 102, 104-105, 108, 109-110, 111, 113-118
Mozart, David (great-great-grandfather), 10
Mozart, Franz (great-grandfather), 10
Mozart, Franz Xaver Wolfgang (son), 114, 116, 118
Mozart, Johann Georg (grandfather), 10
Mozart, Johann Thomas (son), 98, 99, 100
Mozart, Karl Thomas (son), 91, 93, 113, 118
Mozart, Leopold (father), 9-12, 17, 21-29, **30**, 31-34, 37, 39, 40-41, 45-47, 50-56, 58-62, 65, 77-78, 85, 89, 95-96, 99, 102
Mozart, Nannerl (Maria Anna) (sister), 9, 11, 12-13, 16-20, 22, 25, 29, **30**, 34, 40, 45, 48, 49, 52, 62, **71**, 77, 80, 83, 88-91, 96, 99, 118
Mozart, Raimund Leopold (son), 88, 89

124

Mozart, Theresia (daughter), 106, 107
Mozart, Wolfgang Amadeus: birth of, 9;
   baptism, 10; importance of love to, 11-12;
   music lessons, 12-13, 20, 32; music
   compositions of, 13, 28, 32, 35-36, 39, 40,
   43, 45-46, 48-49, 64, 67, 79, 84, 86, 89, 90,
   93, 96, 98, 101, 104, 106, 107, 109, 112, 113-
   116; clavier lessons, 13-14; violin
   lessons/playing, 14, 18, 20; talent of, 16-
   20, 31, 34; tours and performances of, 16-
   29, 33-36, 37-43, 45-49, 52-55, 83, 85-87,
   89, 94, 96, 98, 100-104, 106, 107, 111-115;
   education of, 22; personality of, 54;
   money problems of, 63, 105-110; marriage
   contract, 81-82; wedding, 85; death, 115-
   116; burial, 117-118
Mozart, Wolfgang Amadeus (illustrations):,
   2, 8, 71, 72, 76, 92; with Leopold and
   Nannerl, 30; at Maria Theresa's court,
   Vienna, 44; birthplace of, 70; performing
   with Nannerl, 71; first composition of,
   72; working on the Requiem, 75; grave of,
   75
Munich, 16-17, 22, 48-49, 52-53, 67, 68
Nancy, 65
Naples, 42
National Theater, 65
Nissen, Georg Nikolaus von, 118
Noverre, J.G., 47
Obligation of the First and Foremost
   Commandment, 32
Olomouc, 33
operas, 18, 34-36, 39, 42-43, 46, 48-49, 66-67,
   79, 97-98, 100, 101, 104, 106, 109, 115
oratorio, 32
organ 22
Padua, 43
Paisiello, Giovanni, 97
Papal Choir, 41
Papal Order of the Golden Spur, 42, 76
Paris, 24-26, 58-60, 63-65
Paris symphony, 64

Parma, 40
Passau, 17
Paula, Hieronymus Joseph Franz von, 46
pet starling, 93, 102
Philharmonic Academy, 42
piano concertos, 49, 93, 96, 112
pianoforte, 60
Piccinni, Niccolò, 59
Pompadour, Madame, 25
Potsdam, 107
Prague, 100, 101, 103, 104, 107, 114, 117-118
Prater, 87
Pressburg, 20
Pretended Garden-Girl, 48, 49
Pretended Simpleton, The, 35, 36
prompter, 57
Puchberg, Michael, 106, 108
Ramm, 55-56
Raaff, Anton, 55
recitatives, 114
Requiem, 115-116, 118-119
Rome, 41
Rovereto, 39
Rudolph, 60
Saint Eustache, Cemetery of, 63
Saint Gilgen, 90
Saint Mark's Cemetery, 117
Saint Nicholas's Church, 118
Saint Stephen's Cathedral, 18
Saint Thomas's Church, 108
Salieri, Antonio, 82, 109, 113, 115, 116
Salomon, Johann Peter, 112
Salzburg, 9, 17, 18, 20, 24, 28, 29, 31-32, 36,
   46, 47, 49, 54, 58, 66, 70, 77, 84-85, 88, 89,
   118
Sammartini, Giovanni Battista, 39
San Marco, Monastery of, 39
Schikaneder, Emanuel, 112, 113
Schmeling, Gertrud Elisabeth, 16
Schönbrunn Palace, 19, 20
Schrattenbach, Count Sigismund von, 10
Schwetzingen, 22

serenades, 49, 84
serenatas, 45-46
Shaw, George Bernard, 117
Sigismund, Prince-Archbishop, 31, 36, 46
"singet dem Herrn," 108
Singspiel, 79
singplay, 79
smallpox, 33
Soler, Vincente Martín y, 98
sonatas, 26, 28, 49, 66, 79, 89, 90, 101, 109
Sonnenburg, Baron Berchtold von, 90
Stadler, Anton, 115
Stephanie, Gottlieb, 79
Storace, Nancy, 93, 98, 101
Storace, Stephen, 93, 101
Strasbourg, 65
string quartets, 40, 90
string quintets, 101, 109, 112
Süssmayr, Franz, 114, 116, 118
Swieten, Baron Gottfried van, 86, 107, 117
symphonies, 18, 28, 35, 48, 64, 66, 100-101, 107
Thekla, Maria Anna (Bäsle), 53-54, 65
Theodor, Elector Palatine Carl, 22
Thorwart, Johann von, 81, 85
Thun, Count Johann Joseph, 90, 100
travel conditions, 16-17

Turin, 43
typhus, 29
Venice, 43
"Veni sancte spiritus," 35
Verona, 39, 43
Versailles, 25, 60
Vicenza, 43
Victoire, Madame, 26
Vienna, 17-18, 33-34, 47, 68, 77-79, 82, 85-88, 95-97, 112-113, 115, 119
violin lessons/playing, 14, 18, 20
Wagenseil, Georg Christoph, 34
Waldstädten, Baroness von, 85, 86
Walsegg-Stuppach, Count Franz von, 113
Wasserburg, 22
Weber, Aloysia, 57-59, 61, 64, 66, 77-78
Weber, Constanze. (*See* Mozart, Constanze Weber)
Weber, Fridolin, 58, 77
Weber, Josefa, 58, 78
Weber, Maria Cäcilie, 77, 78, 83, 85, 88
Weber, Sophie, 78, 85, 116
Weigl, Joseph, 109
Wendling, Johann Baptist, 55-56
Wieden, Theater auf der, 112
Wunderkinder, 15-20
Zeil, Prince, 52

126

ABOUT THE AUTHOR

Carol Greene has degrees in English literature and musicology. She has worked in international exchange programs, as an editor, and as a teacher. She now lives in St. Louis, Missouri, and writes full time. She has had over fifty books published, most of them for children. Other Childrens Press biographies by Ms. Greene include *Louisa May Alcott*, *Marie Curie*, *Thomas Alva Edison*, *Hans Christian Andersen*, and *Marco Polo* in the People of Distinction series, and *Sandra Day O'Connor*, *Mother Teresa*, *Indira Nehru Gandhi*, *Diana, Princess of Wales*, *Desmond Tutu*, and *Elie Wiesel* in the Picture-Story Biography series.